Bedtime Stories for Elders

What Fairy Tales Can Teach Us
About the New Aging

Bedtime Stories for Elders

What Fairy Tales Can Teach Us
About the New Aging

Rev. John C. Robinson, PhD., D. Min.

BOOKS

Winchester, UK
Washington, USA

First published by O-Books, 2012
O-Books is an imprint of John Hunt Publishing Ltd., Laurel House, Station Approach,
Alresford, Hants, SO24 9JH, UK
office1@jhpbooks.net
www.johnhuntpublishing.com

For distributor details and how to order please visit the 'Ordering' section on our website.

Text copyright: John C. Robinson 2011

ISBN: 978 1 78099 353 9

A CIP catalogue record for this book is available from the British Library.

Design: Stuart Davies

Printed and bound by CPI Group (UK) Ltd, Croydon, CR0 4YY

We operate a distinctive and ethical publishing philosophy in all
areas of our business, from our global network of authors to
production and worldwide distribution.

CONTENTS

Dedication

To: Agnes Claflin Adams and her friend Periwinkle

Why Fairy Tales?

Our deepest truths are hidden in fairy tales.

I remember my grandmother sitting on the patio of our home in California happily absorbing the winter sun. Looking up from her reading, she began talking to me about fairies, who, she insisted, still lived in the world, including our own garden. But I was ten years old and did not believe in fairies. The fact that she did, however, intrigued me. How could a sixty-three-year-old woman, a real "grown-up," consider such silliness? With my superior knowledge, the conversation did not last long.

My grandmother went on to write a collection of fairy tales for her growing gaggle of grandchildren. I carried her little book of mimeographed stories with me through six cities, four academic degrees, and fifty-five years of life, but never read it. Recently I dug it out of storage and was stunned. Her fairy tales now spoke to me in a completely different way.

My education in fairy tales (and the related genres of myth, parable, fable and legend) began in the mid-1990s when I became involved in the men's movement - a rising up of midlife men frustrated with the exhausting, soul-numbing, competitive model of masculinity championed by popular culture. The requirement to be strong, confident and stoic in the world when feeling compromised, broken or dead inside was both painful and dishonest. Deep in the Mendocino redwoods of northern California, we came together as men to acknowledge our wounds and explore an alternative vision of manhood, one surprisingly sourced from ancient stories.

Spread across the daily story-telling portion of these retreats, a single fairy tale or myth would galvanize the gathering for a week, holding each man spellbound as he discovered his own personal connection to its remarkable wisdom. Building on the profound understanding of symbols advanced by the psychoanalyst Carl Jung, mythologist Joseph Campbell, drumming story-teller Michael Mead, poet Robert Bly, and Jungian analysts James Hillman, Robert Johnson, and Allan Chinen, we learned to access the wisdom of these stories in new ways. The Rosetta Stone of depth psychology uncovered insights of timeless value. It was amazing!

I learned much from the teachers of story and myth. I learned that a simple fairy tale, told over and over across the centuries in the oral tradition preceding the printing press, collected the wisdom and experience of each generation, its symbolism growing ever more profound with time. I learned, too, that we each held a piece of the puzzle, for as we explored our own personal meanings, we were uncovering the story's deeper arche-typal ones. Interpreted symbolically, fairy tales taught us about men and masculinity, women and femininity, and the great adventures of love, sorrow, death and transformation. They nourished every nook and cranny of the tired soul, restoring not only our humanity but, as we will see, our path to divinity as well. And for me, they met a particularly deep and unusual need.

Since my earliest years, I had been studying the psyche, my own and others'. Turning psychological observations and insights over and over in my mind as a lapidary tumbler polishes stones, I kept looking into the hidden depth and nature of the personality. Of course a child does not understand such a quest – it is only truly appreciated looking back, but for me, the search was always present, growing clearer with each decade. Then, in the swirling and painful chaos of midlife, I listened to Robert Bly explain the symbolism of Iron John and Michael Meade unwrap the deep meanings of The Spirit in the Bottle (fairy tales from the Brothers Grimm) and my mind exploded with the insights hidden in these tales.

Suddenly I saw how fairy tale, myth, fable, legend and parable – and for that matter, poetry, novels, movies and life itself, spontaneously express the same unconscious themes in myriad and protean ways, constantly renewing humankind's universal motifs of ultimate meaning. I began to understand the "purpose" of relationship struggles, emotional wounding, and the long journey of life in a new way. As a clinical psychologist, I had been given theories and diagnostic categories for comprehending the emotional problems of life – heady and scientific; now I accessed the far deeper symbolic significance of these problems.

Fairy tales and myths became my new diagnostic manual, and for me they made so much more sense than the medical model. It was glorious. I saw how we must all go out into the world like the Prodigal Son, face the death of the hero like Prometheus, and finally mature like Abraham and Moses to a greater understanding of life in old age. Long interested in spiritual growth, I was disappointed to find very few fairy tales describing enlightened aging. Indeed Alan Chinnen discovered that elder stories comprised less than two percent of all fairy tales, suggesting that humankind really has very little experience with old age, which is not surprising when we recall the average life span in the middle ages was twenty-five (it reached forty-five in 1900 and sixty-five when the baby boomers came along). Living now into our mid-seventies and eighties, however, has created a new aging experience but we need new elder tales to fill the void.

Bedtime Stories for Elders is built upon ten profound and powerful stories revealing the unseen psychological and spiritual dimensions of this new aging, providing a lens through which our own aging will make more sense. With each tale, we travel more deeply into the ultimate meaning and transformational potential of aging. Enjoy these tales but do not rush through them – profound teachings take a long time to digest. Instead, take one story at a time, imagine yourself as the protagonist, carry the story around for several days and let it work in your unconscious, stirring up imagination, dreams, and unexpected insights. For me, this deep absorption in fairy tales is more than an academic exercise, it has become a spiritual practice, and I find it fascinating that we can return to the world's fairy tales in old age to discover their ultimate wisdom. I encourage you to apply this wisdom to your own life, for the real gold nuggets glitter there.

Finally, don't be fooled by the apparent simplicity, superficiality or strange symbolism of fairy tales – they are profound and powerful beyond measure. Even more amazing, like Russian nesting dolls, this book is made of story within story within story, and the most fantastic may just be true. So here is my guarantee: understood deeply, these fairy tales will change you. And for those wishing additional guidance on interpreting fairy tales, please consult the Appendix. Once on board, you can journey on your own into the deep and shining wisdom of fairy tales.

The Little Elder-Tree Mother

Dreaming the Adventure of Life

Our first fairy tale invites us to understand the journey of life from an entirely new perspective. It begins with a little boy in bed with a cold brought on by an adventure with water. By the end of this charming and beautiful tale, we will learn something about the Elder's gift to humanity and the universal dream of life that we all make our own.

There was once a little boy who had caught cold; he had gone out and got his wet feet. Nobody had the least idea how it had happened; the weather was quite dry. His mother undressed him, put him to bed, and ordered the teapot to be brought in, that she might make him a good cup of tea from the elder tree blossoms, which is so warming. At the same time, the kind-hearted old man who lived by himself in the upper storey of the house came in; he led a lonely life, for he had no wife and children; but he loved the children of others very much, and he could tell so many fairy tales and stories, that it was a pleasure to hear him.

"Now, drink your tea," said the mother; "perhaps you will hear a story."

"Yes, if I only knew a fresh one," said the old man, and nodded smilingly. "But how did the little fellow get his wet feet?" he then asked.

"That," replied the mother, "nobody can understand."

"Will you tell me a story?" asked the boy.

"Yes, if you can tell me as nearly as possible how deep is the gutter in the little street where you go to school."

"Just half as high as my top-boots," replied the boy; "but then I must stand in the deepest holes."

"There, now we know where you got your wet feet," said the old

5

man. "I ought to tell you a story, but the worst of it is, I do not know any more."

"You can make one up," said the little boy. "Mother says you can tell a fairy tale about anything you look at or touch."

"That is all very well, but such tales or stories are worth nothing! No, the right ones come by themselves and knock at my forehead saying: 'Here I am.'"

"Will not one knock soon?" asked the boy; and the mother smiled while she put elder tree blossoms into the teapot and poured boiling water over them. "Pray, tell me a story."

"Yes, if stories came by themselves; they are so proud, they only come when they please. But wait," he said suddenly, "there is one. Look at the teapot; there is a story in it now."

And the little boy looked at the teapot; the lid rose up gradually, the elder tree blossoms sprang forth one by one, fresh and white; long boughs came forth; even out of the spout they grew up in all directions, and formed a bush—nay, a large elder tree, which stretched its branches up to the bed and pushed the curtains aside; and there were so many blossoms and such a sweet fragrance! In the midst of the tree sat a kindly-looking old woman with a strange dress; it was as green as the leaves, and trimmed with large white blossoms, so that it was difficult to say whether it was real cloth, or the leaves and blossoms of the elder tree.

"What is this woman's name?" asked the little boy.

"Well, the Romans and Greeks used to call her a Dryad," said the old man; "but we do not understand that. Out in the sailors' quarter they give her a better name; there she is called Elder-Tree Mother. Now, you must attentively listen to her and look at the beautiful elder tree."

The Elder-Tree Mother spoke for the first time. "Real life furnishes us with subjects for the most wonderful fairy tale," she said, "for otherwise my beautiful elder bush could not have grown forth out of the teapot!"

And then the ELDER-TREE MOTHER took the little boy out of

bed and held him close; the elder branches, full of blossoms, closed over them; it was as if they sat in a thick leafy bower which flew with them through the air; it was beautiful beyond all description. The little Elder-Tree Mother had suddenly become a charming young girl, but her dress was still of the same green material, covered with white blossoms, as the Elder-Tree Mother had worn; she had a real elder blossom on her bosom, and a wreath of the same flowers was wound round her curly golden hair; her eyes were so large and so blue that it was wonderful to look at them. She and the boy were now the same age and felt the same joys. They walked hand in hand out of the bower, and now stood at home in a beautiful flower garden.

Near the green lawn the father's walking-stick was tied to a post. There was life in this stick for the little ones, for as soon as they seated themselves upon it the polished knob turned into a neighing horse's head, a long black mane was fluttering in the wind, and four strong slender legs grew out. The animal was fiery and spirited; they galloped round the lawn. "Hooray! Now we shall ride far away, many miles!" said the boy. "We shall ride to the nobleman's estate where we were last year." And they rode round the lawn again, and the little girl, who, as we know, was no other than the little Elder-Tree Mother, continually cried, "Now we are in the country! Do you see the farmhouse there, with the large baking stove, which projects like a gigantic egg out of the wall into the road?

"It is beautiful here in spring," said the little girl, and they were again in the green beechwood, where the thyme breathed forth sweet fragrance at their feet, and the pink anemones looked lovely in the green moss. "Oh! That it were always spring in the fragrant beechwood!"

"Here it is splendid in summer!" she said, and they passed by old castles of the age of chivalry. The high walls and indented battlements were reflected in the water of the ditches, on which swans were swimming and peering into the old shady avenues. The corn waved in the field like a yellow sea. Red and yellow flowers grew in the ditches, wild hops and convolvuli in full bloom in the hedges. In the evening the moon rose, large and round, and the hayricks in the meadows smelt sweetly. "One can never forget it!"

"Here it is beautiful in autumn!" said the little girl, and the atmosphere seemed twice as high and blue, while the wood shone with crimson, green, and gold. The hounds were running off, flocks of wild fowl flew screaming over the barrows, while the bramble bushes twined round the old stones. The dark-blue sea was covered with white-sailed ships, and in the barns sat old women, girls, and children picking hops into a large tub; the young ones sang songs, and the old people told fairy tales about goblins and sorcerers. It could not be more pleasant anywhere.

"Here it's agreeable in winter!" said the little girl, and all the trees were covered with hoar-frost, so that they looked like white coral. The snow creaked under one's feet, as if one had new boots on. One shooting star after another traversed the sky. In the room the Christmas tree was lit, and there were songs and merriment. In the peasant's cottage the violin sounded, and games were played for apple quarters; even the poorest child said, "It is beautiful in winter!"

And indeed it was beautiful! And the little girl showed everything to the boy, and the elder tree continued to breathe forth sweet perfume, while the red flag with the white cross was streaming in the wind. The boy became a youth; he was to go out into the wide world, far away to the countries where the coffee grows. But at parting the little girl took an elder blossom from her breast and gave it to him as a keepsake. He placed it in his prayer-book, and when he opened it in distant lands it was always at the place where the flower of remembrance was lying; and the more he looked at it the fresher it became, so that he could almost smell the fragrance of the woods at home. He distinctly saw the little girl, with her bright blue eyes, peeping out from behind the petals, and heard her whispering, "Here it is beautiful in spring, in summer, in autumn, and in winter," and hundreds of pictures passed through his mind.

Thus many years rolled by. He had now become an old man, and was sitting, with his old wife, under an elder tree in full bloom. They held each other by the hand and talked about bygone days and of their golden wedding anniversary. Now the little girl with the blue eyes and elder blossoms in her hair was sitting high up in the tree, and nodded to them, saying, "Today is your golden wedding!" And then she took two flowers out of her wreath and kissed them. They glittered at first like silver, then like gold, and when she placed them on the heads of the old people each flower became a golden crown. There they both sat like a king and queen under the sweet-smelling tree, which looked exactly like an elder tree, and he told his wife the story of the Elder-Tree Mother as it had been told him when he was a little boy. They were both of opinion that the story contained many points like their own, and these similarities they liked best.

"Yes, so it is," said the little girl in the tree. "Some call me Little Elder-Tree Mother; others a Dryad; but my real name is 'Remembrance.' It is I who sit in the tree which grows and grows. I can remember things and tell stories! But let's see if you have still got your flower."

And the old man opened his prayer-book; the elder blossom was still in it, and as fresh as if it had only just been put in. Remembrance nodded, and the two old people, with the golden crowns on their heads, sat in the glowing evening sun. They closed their eyes and — and —

Well, now the story is ended! The little boy in bed did not know whether he had dreamt it or heard it told; the teapot stood on the table, but no elder tree was growing out of it, and the old man who had told the story was on the point of leaving the room, and he did go out.

"How beautiful it was!" said the little boy. "Mother, I have been to warm countries!"

"I believe you," said the mother; "if one takes two cups of hot elder tea it is quite natural that one gets into warm countries!" And she covered him up well, so that he might not take cold. "You have slept soundly while I was arguing with the old man whether it was a story or a fairy tale!"

"And what has become of the little Elder-Tree Mother?" asked the boy.

"She is in the teapot," said the mother; "and there she may remain."

Interpretation

A bored little boy in bed with a cold, his loving mother, a kindly Elder known as a skilled storyteller, and the mystery of how the child got his feet wet on a dry day, begin this tale – in the world of fairy tales, it's a recipe for enchantment. Strangely the mother does not ask her son how his feet got wet – she is more concerned with cure than etiology – but she has the innate wisdom to bring him into the realm of the Elder – through the elder tree tea she serves and the old man from above who told a story that came knocking on his forehead.

Employing his quiet wisdom, the Elder easily solves the mystery of the wet feet with a clever question and the boy inadvertently reveals his budding penchant for stepping into the deep. The Elder then fascinates the boy with his explanation of how stories arise, emphasizing that real fairy tales are not concocted intentionally but visit spontaneously of their own accord from the other world, an explanation that quickly evokes the boy's – and the reader's – interest, anticipation and imagination. Connecting the mother's elder tree tea with the sudden arrival of a new tale, the Elder begins weaving the magic spell of storytelling. He is going to feed this boy's hunger for the wisdom of deep places, a reference to humanity's collective unconscious.

This story centers on the Tree of Life, a symbol of the rich diversity of the human experience through the seasons (later we will explore its place in the mythical Garden of Eden). While variations in our individual experiences are endless, the basic themes remain eternal – mothers, fathers, siblings, love, adventure, betrayal, loss, struggle, divinity, aging and death. From this universal template of branching possibilities, we each grow a tree of our own full of gifts. But there's more to this particular tree.

Common to the British Isles, the elder tree has long been known for the cornucopia of gifts flowing through its leaves, flowers, berries and bark. These gifts include herbal tea to sooth and cure colds, sore throats, flu and rheumatism; elderberry wine for ritual and celebration; wood for carving combs, flutes and children's toys; and, hung in doorways, a way to bless a house or ward off evil spirits. Because of these gifts, the elder tree in particular symbolizes the creative power of the life – a profound and sacred gift given to each of us. And because of its name, this symbol also suggests that this story may be about receiving the wisdom gifts of age.

British folk tales further speak of the Elder-Tree Mother who lives among its branches to protect and bless those below. She is the third form of the triple goddess – maiden, mother and crone – and can, as the story illustrates, change appearance easily, symbolizing the shape-shifting mystery of the feminine through the life span. Her power comes from the role she already plays in the little boy's unconscious.

Psychologically, the triple goddess represents the anima, a term the psychoanalyst Carl Jung used to describe the inner feminine image and consciousness residing in a man's unconscious. She embodies his capacity for love, intuition, and caretaking. A man unconsciously projects this part of himself onto the woman he loves, romanticizing her as the soul-mate needed to complete his wholeness, just as a woman projects her animus (the masculine capacity for forceful action, singularity of purpose, and tribal defense) onto the man she loves in search of the same union. In essence, anima or animus symbolize the missing part of the self that we long to experience, embrace and express. No wonder the anima or animus projection holds the powerful allure associated with romantic love.

In fairytale and myth, the anima also serves as guide to the depths of the unconscious, like Dante's Beatrice. Because she dwells in his unconsciousness, she leads him into himself, stirring the deep call of love, the great adventure of individuation (he'll do virtually anything for her love), and, in the end, as he withdraws this projection and recognizes the anima as part of his own nature, the ripening of wisdom. All this is what the little shape-shifting elder-Tree Mother symbolizes – virtually the divine feminine in her myriad forms, and this is why she can enchant the boy, evoke the dream of his life, and then become the soul-mate needed to reflect his potential wholeness. She is, in essence, his own soul and he unconsciously seeks her everywhere. And most remarkably, all this is already in the boy's psyche waiting to be evoked through the events and stages of life, which is why she can reveal the dream of his life before he has lived it!

The boy in the story, of course, represents youth, a time when we prepare to embark on the great journey of life. With her magic, the Elder-Tree Mother shows him the fiery instinctual energies of youth, symbolized by the powerful play horse that turns into a stallion and the marvelous adventures he will pursue before settling down. She also illuminates the beauty of the four seasons – of the year and of life itself – and, at the end of the story, shape-shifts into the crone whose wisdom comes from remembrance. Bracketed between callow youth and wise old age, this story within a story weaves the whole fabric of life.

But what is this life the boy has seen? His mother argues with the storyteller, debating whether the story was a dream, a fantasy, a fairy tale, a prophecy, or an actual life preview. While we can defend each assertion, in truth, it is all of them. It is the flowering of the Tree of Life hidden within, and each of us will live our unique variation of its universal themes. We all fall short of the romantic perfection described in this particular tale, for our wounds, mistakes and disappointments seem to represent places where the story failed us – but these, too, are part of the universal tale, often revealing our greatest lessons and gifts. Getting off course encourages us to find our way back; the pain of wounding opens us to the inner life where meaning dwells, and failure teaches us not to identify completely with heroic fantasies. Never be afraid to fail, my father's father told him, for failure is how we learn.

The story reveals one more precious thing about aging, specifically: the Elder's wisdom is born of remembrance, the final review and understanding of the universal story summarized in our own unique life. Remembrance is the aging self reflecting sentimentally on life's meaning, beauty and "rightness" in spite of all. Whether wise old man or crone, the Elder who knows Remembrance speaks with the wisdom of the ages and kindness of the saint.

Conclusions

In the form of a fairy tale, a young boy is given an amazing preview of his life all the way to old age. Though he is too young to understand what he was shown, one day he will realize that the story really came from him – it was stored in his psyche all along waiting to be projected onto the world and experienced as his own life. As we all do, he travels the long and winding road from tender child to adventure-seeking youth, from first love to family, from loss and struggle to wisdom. Each step is a uniquely configured universal experience; each initiates a new stage, transforms his psyche, and reveals a new world.

At the end of the story-within-a-story, the old man holds his prayer book with the elder tree blossom still in it, symbolizing the holiness of this final time and the sacred gift of remembrance he received. Then the old couple closes their eyes, but the sentence goes unfinished. We naturally assume death has come but all that really happens is that the story ends. This is a tantalizing ambiguity, for as we will later see, perhaps there is another possibility.

Reflections

As an eight-year-old, I remember playing for hours along side my older brother in a water-filled sandbox building islands, roads, bridges and towns; building my life. I remember dressing up as a policeman, a cowboy, and a football player in costumes from a toy store catalogue, trying out different versions of manhood. I remember lying in bed as a preadolescent daydreaming about a girl in elementary school who seemed to be everything I ever wanted, and writing an autobiography in the seventh grade – a curious homework assignment for a 13-year-old! – picturing how I would be just like my father when I grew up. In later adolescence, I imagined myself as a psychologist, understanding the secret workings of the psyche. All along, of course, I really just wanted to be my self but needed these experimental variations to see which branch felt right; it was like trying on clothes. Though I sometimes felt that I would never find my real work or deep love, I always returned to my quest, and eventually found them both.

Looking back, I see how fresh, sensory and tender life was in springtime, how determined I was in summer, how introspective at midlife and soulful in fall, and now, how reflective I am looking backwards, searching for meaning, in order to go forward to the end. I see how profoundly the shape-shifting goddess touched my story and how much I learned about her love over the past six decades. It was all there, all waiting to come out, all part of me already, needing to be felt and lived. Though I could never have imagined the life I actually led, the friends I have found, the many wounds I sustained and the precious family that has grown around me, I always sensed its necessary outlines and felt the absolute imperative of finding a life I could call my own. I am still on my own path as I move into the mystery of old age.

Your Story

To encourage your own reflections, I will ask you questions at the end of each story to evoke your connection to its themes. Here are some questions that might open new depths of insight and understanding of your own psychological development. Reflecting on your own story...

How were you eager as a child to begin the adventure of life? Did you lie on the grass in summertime opening your stored fantasies to preview your life? What adventures did you anticipate?

Looking back from wherever you currently are, and looking around at the lives of others, can you see how we all live the same seasons of life with the same energies, dreams, wounds and, with luck, the same eventual wisdom of remembrance? What season are you in now?

How is remembrance turning into wisdom for you? Where are you applying this wisdom? What have you learned so far about the universal story of life and your own version of it?

King O'Toole and His Goose

Coming of Age

A whimsical adventure from the Celtic tradition, our next story provides some remarkable wisdom on aging. Like the old couple in The Little Elder-Tree Mother, our protagonist has entered the final season of life but, unlike that idealized pair, his road is bumpier for, like the rest of us, he must deal with a variety of very real problems and losses associated with old age and death. Curiously, the King appears to have no feminine figure to guide him, or does he?

In the long ago past of Ireland, in another time, in a time before this time, there lived a King named O'Toole, and a fine king he was. He supported the parishes in his kingdom, lived his life fully, and most of all loved the hunting sport. In the years of his prime, off he'd be riding in the valleys and the mountains of the land, from sun up to sun down, and fine times they were for this jolly and portly prince.

But in the way of all things, time eventually changed the king. His body grew old, his limbs stiffened, and one day even his heart failed him. Stricken, he had no choice but to give up the hunting life, and a mighty sad day it was.

For want of sport and diversion, the poor old king at last took on a goose. A goose, you say? What need a king of a goose? But 'tis the truth I'm telling you, and the king loved to watch his goose swim across the lake, dive for trout, and bring him a fish every Friday night for dinner. Every other day, the goose would fly completely around round the lake, thrilling the crippled old monarch with her sporting ways.

Well the old king was happily diverted like this for some years. But eventually, the goose got old, too, just like her master, and could no longer fill his life with sport and diversion. It was a cruel, cruel ending, the King lamented, and one day he approached the edge of the lake with the thought of throwing himself into its cold, dark waters. Just as he turned to face the bitter end, the king spied a fair young man, modest in dress and manner, who approached him directly.

"God save you," said the king to the stranger.

"And God save you, King O'Toole," said the young man.

Startled, the King replied, "Surely, I am King O'Toole, the sovereign prince of these seven parishes, but how came ye to know me?"

"Oh, never you mind," answered St. Kevin, who was himself the great Irish saint in disguise. "But may I inquire about your goose, King O'Toole?"

"Och," cried the king, "How do you know of my goose?"

"It matters not," replied the young man, "but I am an honest man who earns his keep by making old things new again."

"A tinker you say?" asked the king.

"No itinerant mender of pots and kettles am I," said the young man, "but what say you if I could make your goose as good as new?"

Well, no one in all the lands could have spoken happier words to the king, who instantly whistled for his goose. Like a loyal hound dog, the crippled old bird waddled over to her master, and St. Kevin could see how they were alike as peas in a pod, and so he said,

"I'll do it."

"And if you do," cried the king, "you will be the cleverest fellow in all these parts."

"But," said the young man, "you must offer more than praise for this deed. What will ye give to have this goose be good as new?"

"Anything ye ask," replied the king without hesitation, "Anything at all."

"Now that's the way to bargain!" the young man said, "but here is the final price. Will you surrender to me all the countryside the goose flies over on her first jaunt after I make her new again?"

And again, without hesitation, the king replied, "I will indeed!"

"Then it's a bargain," said St. Kevin, and he picked up the poor

old goose by her wings, made the sign of the cross, and threw her into the air. Miraculously, this tired old bird was new again, flying swift as an eagle, darting like a swallow, and happy as a lark. A soft rain fell from the heavens as the goose landed at the king's feet.

"And what do ye say, King O'Toole," asked the young man.

"I say 'tis a blessed day that my goose flies again."

"And what else do ye say?"

"I say you are the cleverest lad in all the world."

"Ah, but what of our bargain?" persisted St. Kevin. "Am I given all the territory your goose just flew over? Will you keep your promise to me?"

"Yes," replied the king. And you're welcome to it though it's my entire kingdom and all I have left."

Then St. Kevin said to the king, "Tis a wise man you are, King O'Toole, for if you had not kept your bargain, the devil himself would have bit your goose and he'd never fly again."

Now St. Kevin was well pleased with the king, and finally revealed his true identity. The king dropped to his knees and paid the proper respect. Then at last St. Kevin explained, "I came here to test you, King O'Toole. And you were a true and decent man. You may stay on your land and I will support you."

And so the king's beloved goose was returned to him, good as new, giving him pleasure every day until he died. On that fateful Friday, the goose dived into the lake after a trout, struck an eel instead, and died instantly. The eel, however, would not eat the goose for the fear of anything the blessed St. Kevin had touched. And so ends the story of King O'Toole and his Goose.

Interpretation

By the implied age of the king and his failing health, we know that this is a winter's tale. The themes of aging, death and resurrection suggest a religious parable about the transformational power of loss, faith, and sincerity.

To understand the symbolic wisdom of this story, let's begin with our protagonist. King O'Toole represents "everyman," the common experience each of us faces approaching old age. But as a king, he also represents something larger. According to the ancients, the king was the link between God and man and his behavior mediated the fortunes of his kingdom and its people. In mythology, if the king were moral and just, his kingdom thrived. If he were corrupt, on the other hand, crops failed, epidemics and famines ravaged the land, and the people suffered. To be a wise and mature king meant to know and accept this great responsibility. King O'Toole represents the part of us that faithfully carries the responsibility for our own kingdom of family, home, community, and soul.

It may surprise the reader to discover that the goose symbolizes the king's soul, his feminine side. Why? First, with its portly carriage, jolly waddle, and sporting ways, the goose looks and acts just like the king, clearly reflecting his essential nature. Second, the goose is female. As we saw earlier, the soul as anima is typically cast as the opposite sex to the protagonist. Because she helps the king soar free of his aging body, the goose also reflects the realm of imagination and intuition, commonly viewed as the inner realm inhabited by the soul. Finally, flying birds like this one symbolize a capacity to move between Heaven and Earth, yet another quality of soul. It is to his soul, therefore, that King O'Toole wisely turns when his body begins to fail, and she serves him well.

King O'Toole's declining health and related heart attack begin his Road of Trials. As a very physical individual, his increasing physical limitations constitute especially painful losses. Searching for renewal in the wilderness of his suffering, however, the king happily discovers his feminine soul, projected onto the goose. It is as if the terrible loss of his old life had opened him to the possibilities of a more spiritual experience. The absence of other people in this story additionally suggests that it is mostly about the king's inner life.

The goose's exploits on the lake soon bring King O'Toole in touch with the collective unconscious. Because they are deep and unfathomable, large bodies of water in fairy tales and myths often represent the collective unconscious, the repository of humanity's recurring experiences across eons of evolutionary time. These flights of the king's soul thus show him the breadth and depth of the unconscious, and bring him nourishing gifts - profound images, symbols and insights - from its depths. The story's reference to eating a trout every Friday introduces the more distinctly Catholic practice prevalent in Ireland at the time of this latest telling and it will be further recalled that fish are a symbol of Jesus, the fisherman of men. In sum, the king's aging has become an implicit vision quest, a search for new meaning and purpose from the archetypal deep.

The king's willingness to change his behavior indicates that he is beginning to work on the inner tasks of aging – the adjustments of behavior, attitude, and expectation we all make in this final time. He readily surrenders his past life and identity, for neither his sporting life nor regal role now occupy center place in his thoughts. He then works through and survives the suffering associated with these losses, turning to his soul to help him move from the objective physical world of sporting adventures to the inner qualitative world of eternal values, like goodness, generosity, wisdom and love. We can see now that the king's heart attack introduced a new and much needed spiritual stage of life, but his initiation is still incomplete.

Eventually King O'Toole's suffering returns, for the goose, too, grows old and frail. In other words, the time comes when even the soul grows weary of the world. She knows it is time to move on. In his acute grief about the nearness of death, the king confuses the symbolic and the real, and concludes that he must literally throw himself into the lake to die. At the moment of greatest despair, when the cry for meaning and vision are the most heart-felt, the divine responds.

St. Kevin represents God in this story, and more specifically, the spirit of death who approaches us disguised as a symptom, illness, accident, premonition, lament, or dream to initiate us into this new and final stage of growth. Symbolically, St. Kevin offers to heal the king's soul if he willingly gives up all worldly attachments and possessions, which is, of course, the quintessential pre-requisite for initiation, enlightenment, and transformation. The king's spiritual growth becomes evident in his trusting attitude toward St. Kevin, for he immediately sees the validity of surrendering worldly things for the value of spiritual growth. The king has passed the test of initiation. Transcending material attachments, his soul is free to soar again implicitly anticipating its flight into the next world.

What does the eel represent? The eel, too, resides in the collective unconscious and may symbolize the primordial life force of the *kundalini*, the cosmic energy of divinity coiled in the unconscious depths of the personality described in Hindu mythology. As no mortal can directly absorb that much power – like touching a live power line! – the goose dies. Because snakes shed their old skin for a new one, the eel also represents the theme of death and resurrection that occurs exactly where it should in the story (and naturally on a Friday!). And having made his peace with God, the king's soul is protected from harm.

Conclusions

King O'Toole retired easily and successfully after his heart attack, surrendering the identity and activities of his adult years for a new, pleasurable and highly symbolic friendship with his goose. Many people do the same, replacing their work lives with other satisfying interests or activities. But retirement is not initiation nor is it the end of adjustments. For his initiation, King O'Toole needed an encounter with the reality of death. By his sincere surrender to the power and wisdom of the divine, King O'Toole completed his initiation into aging, allowing him to move toward death with faith and acceptance. We do not know what King O'Toole did with the gifts of initiation he received, for this fairy tale dealt primarily with the role of death and divinity in the initiation of age, but we do know that this encounter led to a profound transformation of his relationship to self, soul, and transcendent values.

King O'Toole and His Goose reveals the major psychological and spiritual steppingstones of traditional aging, that is, aging as we understand it so far in our spiritual evolution, so it is good place to get our bearings. But we will also discover that there is another stage of aging extending beyond the traditional into a new dimension of consciousness that will change us, and the world. By surrendering health, rank, and wealth without bitterness or regret, King O'Toole entered this new stage; unfortunately the story does not tell us much about what happened next, though later stories will. For now, it is enough to recognize how death initiated King O'Toole, this jolly symbol of Everyman.

Reflections

Like King O'Toole, a heart crisis led to my premature retirement. Disguised as a medical problem, the spirit of death asked me to surrender my profession to rekindle my soul. As you will see, it presented a nearly incomprehensible initiation for me.

Closing my clinical psychology practice left an enormous hole in my life: what I had done for three decades, I could do no more. Knowing I needed a renewed source of meaning and creativity, I returned to school and began studying interfaith religion and spirituality. What seemed like a merely logical idea at the time soon restored the tired bird of my soul and she soared through the vast and mysterious realms of the world's religions – Judaism, Christianity, Hinduism, Islam, Buddhism, Taoism, Shinto, indigenous spirituality, New Thought, and Paganism, in search of the ultimate meaning of existence. Eventually settling in the nest of an interfaith seminary, I was ordained as an interfaith minister and turned my sights to the transformational possibilities of aging, for after all, I was living it firsthand.

Aging became my soul's new home and the insights she now brought me were indeed amazing. The eventual success of this journey into aging, however, did not mitigate the suffering I experienced along the way. Stumbling through a wilderness of loss, emptiness, and grief, it took several years to come home.

Your Story

Reflecting on your own story...

Imagine the Story of King O'Toole symbolizes your experience of aging. What specific events have or might correspond to the king's surrender of his former life, taking on a goose, meeting St. Kevin, and the bargain he made at the end of the story?

How might your soul teach you to transcend the losses of aging and the body's physical decline? In other words, what activities will allow your imagination to fly free of the body's limitations (e.g., writing poetry, exploring philosophy, religion, and history, creating art, helping others) to expand your spiritual experience and knowledge?

When your soul finally grows weary of the physical plane, how will you greet God disguised again as an illness or accident, for this final confrontation with Death underlies life's ultimate transformation?

Living the Myth of Inanna
Death and Rebirth

Some of the losses of aging are particularly dramatic and intense, pushing us to the edge of what we can bear, and sometimes beyond, creating an initiation of profound proportions. The death of a spouse, a cancer diagnosis, or a major physical disability may test the strength of our psychic metal. Finding a fairy tale or myth for such an experience can be lifesaving. While the ancient tale recounted below embodies many great themes, it was for me a metaphor for my own initiation into aging, and my own confrontation with the dark abyss of death. Take it in slowly, for it is a deep and complex tale.

Inanna and Ereshkigal are sister goddesses presiding over very different lands. Inanna is Queen of the Heaven and Earth; Ereshkigal is Queen of the Underworld. As the story unfolds, we find Ereshkigal, deep in grief, planning the funeral of her recently killed husband, Gugalanna. But theirs has not been an easy marriage. Gugalanna, formerly known as the "great bull of heaven", had been banished to the Underworld by the gods for assuming various disguises to repeatedly rape his wife. In her great love for him, Ereshkigal, once a goddess of the grain, gave up her earthly realm to join her husband in the under-world where she now rules.

Wishing to attend the funeral of her sister's husband, Inanna, the Queen of Heaven and Earth, dresses in her finest regalia and begins the journey down into the underworld. Recognizing the danger of this descent, she tells her trusted aid, Ninshubur, to seek help from the sky gods if she does not return in three days. And so Inanna's journey begins.

Reaching the first gate to the Underworld, Inanna is asked to identify herself by Neti, the chief gatekeeper of the netherworld. After learning of her intentions, Neti returns to Queen Ereshkigal to describe this strange yet powerful visitor and request instructions. Furious, the Queen demands that her younger sister obey all the decrees and rites pertaining to one entering her realm. Specifically, she must remove one piece of her formal regalia at each of the seven gates until she is stripped naked. Inanna consents and the ritual of descent proceeds. At each gate, she is told to be silent, reminded that the decrees of the nether world were perfect, and then another part of her upper world identity is removed: crown, lapis beads, sparkling stones, breastplate, gold ring, lapis measuring rod, and royal robe. Arriving naked, Inanna bows low before Ereshkigal seated on her throne. Her welcome, however, is this: she is condemned by the Anunnaki (seven judges), "fastened upon by the eye of death", murdered, and her corpse hung on a peg to rot.

When his queen has not returned within the allotted three days, Ninshubur begins an impassioned and painful lament, tearing at his eyes and mouth, and beseeching Enlil, the highest god of sky and Earth, to intercede. Citing Inanna's decision to descend and the decrees of the underworld, Enlil refuses, as does Inanna's own father, Nanna, the moon god. Only Enki, god of water and wisdom, responds to Ninshubur's pleas. Bringing forth dirt from his red-painted fingernail, Enki creates two tiny mourners known as the kalaturru. Genderless creatures, they sneak down into the underworld and find Ereshkigal naked, unkempt, and moaning. Following Enki's directions, the kalaturru exactly mirror her pain and grief. Finally, Ereshkigal ceases her moaning and blesses the kalaturru for their compassion, offering them whatever they desire in gratitude. Their request is Inanna's corpse which they soon restore with food and the water of life. Before Inanna can begin her ascent, however, the Anunnnaki remind her that none who descend to the Underworld leave without providing a substitute to take their place.

Inanna returns to the upperworld through the same seven gates, each time reclaiming the parts of her royal regalia she had surrendered. Following her return, she searches for a substitute accom-

panied by underworld demons who first try to take Ninshubur in her place. Citing his unwavering loyalty and indefatigable efforts on her behalf, Inanna denies them. She also refuses to surrender two other faithful attendants as substitutes. But when she finds her consort, Dumuzi, sitting nobly on his throne, Inanna fastens the eye of death upon him and allows the demons to carry him away. Dumuzi weeps and begs for help from Inanna's brother Utu who transforms him into a snake to assist his escape. Dumuzi's sister, Geshtinanna, then offers to take his place in the underworld. In the end, Inanna decrees that Dumuzi and Geshtinanna will alternate this assignment so that each lives half a year above and below.

Interpretation

Ereshkigal represents that part of the feminine – the archetypal Earth goddess – that has been repeated raped, devalued, and dismissed by the dominant patriarchy ever since warrior tribes invaded Old Europe some 6300 years ago. Written in cuneiform script on clay tablets over 5000 years ago, the Summarian Myth of Inanna is the earliest recorded story of a culture's attempt to image, recover, and heal the divided feminine. Residing deep in the collective unconscious, she bears the rage, humiliation, and suffering of her repeated betrayal. For women, this myth may symbolize and guide the psychotherapeutic journey to recover feminine qualities suppressed by the patriarchy. As a story dating to the earliest agrarian civilizations, it is furthermore one of many archetypal depictions of goddess-as-nature in her seasonal round of death and rebirth. But the significance of this myth for men in general and for me in particular is yet another story.

In the summer of 2000, I began an unexpected, extraordinary, and horrifying descent into the underworld. Like King O'Toole, my initiation assumed the guise of a heart condition. It brought me to the emergency room for cardiac defibrillation, deepened through a long progression of horrifying memories, and eventually consumed my practice, my profession as a clinical psychologist, and my income. What was this descent? It was a journey into the dark netherworld of surgical awareness – I began living the Myth of Inanna.

Surgical awareness happens when anesthesia levels become too light to suppress consciousness but neuromuscular blocking agents prevent the patient from communicating this shocking reality to his doctor. The surgical staff does not know the patient is awake, sentient, and terrified. I was 14 years old, undergoing open-heart surgery for correction of a congenital defect, when I began to feel the surgeon's knife cutting through my chest. After the operation, the whole experience was defensively removed from consciousness to protect the integrity of my young psyche. Forty years to the month later, I experienced a heart arrhythmia requiring cardiac conversion – stopping and resetting the heart with electrical shock – an event that began an inexorable rip tide sucking me down into the dark and frozen depths of my repressed surgical memories. Now, after two years of psychotherapy, countless nightmares, and a major decon-struction of identity, I think I have endured the worst, and still, whenever I talk about this, I cry.

Unlike Inanna, my journey into the netherworld of surgical awareness was neither expected nor chosen, nor was there anyone to run to for help if I failed to return, and a significant part of me did not return. In fact, my experience has more in common with the rape and abduction of Persephone, but there was no Demeter searching frantically for me. Looking back, it feels as if I had been tricked into attending my own funeral.

My original descent was into the abyss of surgical awareness. The first gate to the underworld was the hospital. There I met numerous gatekeepers who decreed that I would surrender my home, my clothes, my control, and my parents (parents did not room with their children in 1960). No one asked my permission. No one asked if I wanted to proceed. I was psychologically stripped naked at the very first gate. Like the Hindu phrase

"Neti, Neti", I was neither this nor that; I was a patient, I was nothing.

The second gate was manned by various anonymous technician/priests who performed strange and terrifying rituals on my body. They drew seven vials of blood from my arms, shaved my hairless chest and groin, taped wires to my body, and then left me alone. As I write this, the computer tells me the sentence is in the passive voice and should be rewritten, but I refuse because by this point my voice was passive.

The third gate opened that night when I could not sleep and was given medication in place of comfort. The darkness came over me quickly and I do not remember being taken to surgery the next morning.

The fourth gate opened with the return of consciousness in a cave of darkness. Strange things were being done to my chest: movement, swabbing, cutting, pulling, jerking, sawing, tugging, tearing; hands inside my chest, inside my heart. Then horror, helplessness, and panic: What's happening? I'm not supposed to be feeling this. It is so cold. I can't move. I can't see. Why are they doing this to me? I am so scared.

The fifth gate opened into unbearable grief: Oh my God! I am shattered, butchered, broken. My soft 14-year-old body splayed open with cold, hard instruments. They did this to a sweet young boy who did nothing wrong. I am dead. I am beyond nothing. Then finally it was over.

It was not over. The sixth gate opened when I was back in surgery to find a bleeder. I am being opened up all over again. Will this ever end? Where is my mother?

At the seventh gate, I awakened to see my mother's face pressed against a small window in the door to my room in the ICU. She looked terrified and anguished. I closed my eyes. I would not give her the comfort of showing that I was OK. My body felt violated and numb. There was a tube coming out the right side of my ribcage, an IV in my left hand, and a long bandage down my chest. I am not OK. I am Frankenstein cut apart and sewn together in ragged pieces. Why did they do this to me? No one answered. I was Ereshkigal enraged. The whole experience sank into the dark abyss of forgetting. I had to get "well." I went home. It was over. In the dark, a corpse was rotting on the peg of a surgeon's scalpel.

In my surgical experience, no aid, friend, or parent cried out for help and the corpse of my shattered self was not restored to life. There was, instead, a long, long silence. Forty years of silence as the unfeeling masculine gods of my psyche refused to help. Then one day, a second descent began and I again passed through the seven gates to the underworld:

In 2000, the quiver of atrial fibrillation in my chest brought me back to the first gate of the hospital. The gatekeeper asked me to identify myself, checked with the medical gods within, and let me pass into the inner sanctum of the ER. Once again, personal identity was erased, replaced with the vacuous title of patient, and I proceeded deeper.

At the second gate, the technician/priests again ministered to my body with IV medicines, x-rays, blood tests, and EKG readings. I was now a body in a soulless land.

At the third gate, the head technician/priest made a pronouncement that filled me with unnatural dread and déjà vu: "We will have to stop and restart your heart with an electrical shock." Immediately my soul felt pulled down into a dark and menacing hole but there was no choice. Like an Aztec sacrificial ritual, where the man sees his heart lifted from his chest before he dies, I knew something terrible was about to happen. With a fast-acting anesthetic in my IV, I entered the dark once again. And somewhere in that darkness the heart shock switched on my body's memory system.

Waking up, I asked the doctor if I'd been converted (the procedure is called cardioversion). The ER doctor quipped, "Yes, you're Jewish." Feeling giddy with relief and gratitude, I thought the drama was over. I had dodged the bullet. But it was not over. A fourth gate now opened into weeks of profound fatigue. Something was terribly wrong. I was not the same person. A dark, ominous shadow moved across my life.

The fifth gate opened into bizarre sensations in my chest – rubbery numbness, pressure, pulling, and cutting – that played over and over like a cellular videotape. I sought psychotherapy. My therapist said, "Close your eyes and go into these sensations" and soon the entire surgical experience took over my body and psyche. I was drawn inexorably downward by an undertow of horrific memories, gruesome nightmares, convulsive sobbing, heart palpitations, and depression. Again I felt like Frankenstein – dissociated and dismembered – and this somatic nightmare went on for months. And I was still descending.

At the sixth gate, I surrendered my practice. I could no longer concentrate or hold other peoples' pain. A high school dream, college major, five years of graduate school, licensure, and nearly three decades of being a psychologist ended. I was stripped of my identity, its story, my community, and my place in the world.

At the seventh gate, my long-term disability carrier sent me for independent medical evaluation. Their consultant concluded none of this could have happened, opining that I just didn't want to work any longer. My income was terminated. This final "eye of death" ended my life as I knew it. I lay naked at the bottom of the abyss. But I was helpless no longer.

In my first surgical descent, I was too young and psychologically unformed to process what had happened in the abyss; instead I instinctively split off the experience in order to survive and continue the developmental tasks of adolescence. I had to grow up. But this second descent was different in ways that allowed me to stay and work in the abyss. As a result, the outcome was also different.

In the second descent, like Inanna, I chose the downward journey. I could have resisted, distancing from my grief and anguish with clinical jargon, viewing it merely as depression of unknown or biochemical origin, and treating it simply with medication. But I didn't. Inanna's journey really began when she heard the sorrowful moans of her sister and began searching for their source and significance. She even agreed to the ritual conditions for entering the underworld that led to suffering more than equal to her sister's. So it was for me: my anima, my own feminine consciousness, like a mother searching for her lost and crying child, intentionally journeyed downward into the netherworld. This time, I could bear the pain. I chose this descent.

And, though stripped naked, I was not defenseless the second time. Three decades of experience in depth psychotherapy accompanied me on this journey – I had been to the abyss countless times with those I had guided. I knew there was a way down and a way back, and that people survived the dark passage. In this regard, Ninshubur represented my own observing ego that stayed above ground, knew I needed help, and secured it from the god of water and wisdom, a wonderful metaphor for the psychotherapist. Though I had first consulted the wrong gods – the patriarchal sky gods of clinical medicine – I now entrusted myself to the anima goddess of the unconscious depths.

Unlike the first descent, when the feminine presence was so profoundly missing from the surgical theater, this time, she accompanied me throughout the underworld journey. My wife remained close to me during the defibrillation procedure, understood and supported my decision to close my practice, and fully stood with me through this time of hardship and transition. The feminine also appeared disguised as my male therapist. Patient and compassionate, he was also the kalaturru who willingly mirrored my unmitigated horror, anguish, and mourning until the corpse was revived. Then there was my mother. As it turned out, her younger brother – my namesake – had died of polio also at the age of 14. At the time of my surgery, she was as paralyzed by fear and unresolved sorrow as I was by anesthetic chemicals, and could not be there for me. In the second descent, long after finally grieving her brother's death, sitting with me in her kitchen, she held my pain with an almost archetypal maternal love. And, lastly, the feminine presence came from myself – my own capacity to listen, love, bear, and nourish my shattered soul.

But the story now has an unexpected twist. No one returns from the underworld without finding a substitute to take his or her place. What does it mean to find a substitute for one's self in the underworld and who should take my place? The myth suggests three fundamentally different meanings and criteria for the selection of a replacement:

Revenge or retaliation: Inanna's search for her substitute became a struggle with the demons of revenge and retaliation who were happy to pick the first man they come upon. And Inanna, too, winds up "fastening the eye of death" on a man – her consort – ostensibly because of his regal detachment. Should I fasten the "eye of death" on the aloof patriarchy of clinical medicine that exiled the feminine presence from the operating theater, surgically annihilated my soul, and then left it for dead? Or, shall I blame my mother (or the feminine in general) for abandoning me throughout my surgical experience? But neither medicine nor my mother was aware of betraying me, and revenge, while tempting, yields little emotional growth or benefit; and after all, the surgery saved my life.

Compassion: All three women in this myth – Ereshkigal, Inanna, and Geshtinanna – voluntarily entered the underworld out of concern and compassion for others. In striking contrast, the two men residing in the underworld - Gugalanna and Dumuzi – were sent there as punishment. This distinction marks a powerful difference between feminine and masculine approaches to justice, that is, between compassion and punishment. Perhaps I should ask one of these women to take my place in order to bring comfort, compassion and consciousness to my inner suffering.

Transformation: The Myth of Inanna is clearly about the descent of the goddess, for this theme is repeated three times. But a journey like this holds different meaning for each gender. For women, the story depicts the exile of the feminine to the collective unconscious and encourages them to heal this split by restoring the deep feminine to their lives. But just as importantly, this story challenges men and the patriarchy to welcome the anima-as-goddess into their interior for the sake of personal and social transformation. If the consciousness of the goddess were to join the deep masculine in the male psyche, what a different world this world be!

Because all the ego's choices reverberate in the unconscious, and because we must personally bear the karmic consequences for the really big decisions, it is extremely important to make a wise selection of one's substitute. After much soul searching, I came to this conclusion: I would select my mother, not with the cold, vengeful "eye of death" but with deep respect for her as a symbol of the inner journey. With her life force dwindling in the twilight descent of congestive heart failure and dementia, my mother has become very soft, almost transparent, infused with new and luminous warmth like a Japanese lantern. I sense that she could bring her light into that dark abyss, transforming my interior, and my aging, with its sacred glow. I always needed more feminine presence in my psyche and now I have it. My mother will move there anyway upon her death.

Conclusions

While the Myth of Inanna contains many archetypal themes, it is most certainly a story of initiation into the mysteries of death and rebirth, for our protagonist must die to her identity, authority, and life in order to awaken renewed and transformed. For me, open-heart surgery, occurring as it did in adolescence and bringing me to the very edge of death, had been a profound but incomplete initiation. As physically and spiritually challenging as any vision quest, there had been no spiritual preparation or community container to guide and bless my descent or welcome me back as a "life bringer." It was, in short, a rite of passage without the rite. Four decades had to pass before this initiation could be resumed and completed in a second descent ritualized this time in personal story, ancient myth, and community sharing.

In this story we again meet the anima as guide, leading the protagonist - me - into the depths of the underworld, into a secret devastation, to find and heal the wounded self. This, too, is part of the aging experience. The great losses of age ask us to journey down into the depths of the underworld to face and heal our wounds, some of them reaching far back into childhood. In this grieving process, we eventually die to the old world in order to enter the new one. This is what King O'Toole was trying to do when he mistakenly began walking into the lake.

In sum, real aging is not as easy as it was for the old couple in The Little Elder-Tree Mother. Death, actual and symbolic, is rarely easy, but it comes with the territory and it has a purpose – it asks us to surrender our former life, heal old wounds, integrate self and soul, and see life anew. For me at the summit of 65 years of age, I now sense the awakening of the anima-goddess-soul inside – for she is the substitute I chose – and look forward to the continuing transformation of consciousness that comes when the divine is invited into the heart.

Reflections

Because this tale so completely absorbed my unconscious, I had to interpret it first as my own story. Only then could I achieve enough emotional distance to see it as an allegory for the losses of aging and the necessary journey into grief we must take in order to heal and grow.

Great losses ask us to descend into the grief and ashes of our woundedness. Grief will not go away by itself. But there is more.

Like Ereshkigal, we have all been hurt by life along the way and the losses of aging often return us to our original wounds. To heal, we must descend into the underworld of repressed memory and emotion, stripping ourselves of our familiar and convenient defenses, and experience both our current and original pain. And like Inanna, worldly success will not protect us. Moreover, something in us must also die in this descent – an old identity, dream, dependency, revenge fantasy, or belief that has protected us from the original hurt. In this kind of allegory, dying means giving up trying to fix the past and instead finally letting our pain and tears come through. And they will. But we can get help along the way, and sometimes this help is critical to our survival and renewal.

For me, this story underscores the powerful encounter with death that is key to the aging process. In a recent men's gathering on aging, I asked the eighty-some participants how many thought frequently about death. For those over 60, nearly all their hands went up. It is as if we know intuitively that death will be the great teacher now – not that dying is imminent, but that the reality and symbolism of death will change us.

I recently met Death in this way and can attest to its power. Out of the blue, I received the kind of wake-up call you get at this age. Routine blood work revealed that my bone marrow was producing abnormal plasma cells, and the process was suggestive of multiple myeloma – a largely incurable bone cancer. For weeks, I underwent endless testing – more blood work, bone marrow biopsy, skeletal x-rays, an MRI – and was referred to a top cancer specialist in Seattle. It was only after he reassured us that the results were benign that my wife and I began to breathe again. Amidst the wild flux of emotions attending this experience, I met Death. It was a very powerful experience: values and priorities became crystal clear, and family and friends were at the top.

Then, in a dream soon thereafter, I saw a boy walking in the desert toward a hole in the ground. It was an underground dwelling. When he reached the hole, a huge balloon appeared over it, inflated by the rushing air from below, becoming a very large and scary-looking black figure that towered above him. But the boy was not particularly afraid; rather he waited until his father came out of the hole. Together they rode a broomstick pulling the black figure with them off into the distance. Upon awakening, I knew immediately that this figure was Death, but he was not scary after all. The wind of fear and anxiety rushing up from inside had inflated this Halloween caricature. On his deathbed years ago, my father told me he was not afraid to die, for he had seen the other side in a vision. He had made peace with Death. This dream was showing me that fear inflates fearful images, that death is not what I thought, and that, with my father's message, I could travel on a witch's broomstick into the future to bring this realization to others.

Your Story

Reflecting on your own story…

Can you recall a time when losses or other life events pulled you down into the underworld of grief, depression, or old wounds? What happened and how did you feel? How did you find your way out?

How have you experienced the reality of personal death in the aging process? How did you feel? How did this experience change you? If you haven't experienced this reality, what do you imagine it will be like?

As a woman, how have you needed to recover your own deep femininity as part of your aging experience? As a man, how have you needed to recover your inner feminine as part of your aging experience? Why might this be important to you?

Nachiketas Meets Death

The Secret of Consciousness

As we have seen, the specter Death plays a pivotal role in elder fairy tales, suggesting that we must understand its nature and purpose to understand aging. So far, our protagonists have met death three times. The old couple in the Elder-Tree Mother, having lived good and full lives, accepted their dying with equanimity but not inquiry. King O'Toole had the maturity to meet Death directly and it changed his life, but he did not ask Death to disclose his secrets. Inanna (and I) returned to tell of the journey of death and rebirth, and much was revealed about this powerful descent, but something was still missing. If facing Death awakens the wisdom of aging, it is time to approach him directly and see what he has to say.

In this next tale, adapted from the Hindu Katha Upanishad, we find our protagonist to be not only pure, brave, and sincere, but determined to wrestle life's ultimate secrets from Death himself. Natchiketas' aged father, a selfish and petty man, thought he could trick the god of death into letting him into Heaven – never a good idea. As Natchiketas learns, a frank and respectful conversation with Death proves the wiser approach. While this story may, at first glance, seem complicated and strange, remember that ancient tales hide their teaching in symbols that are confusing only because our assumptions and beliefs obscure our wisdom.

Vajasravasa, an old cowherder, was planning a ritual sacrifice to the gods. But his heart was insincere, for his sacrifice, based solely on a selfish desire to enter Heaven, consisted of offering to God only old cows too weak and sick even for milk. His young son, Nachiketas, saw this hypocrisy and knew it would lead only to a world of sorrow.

Wishing his father could make a more worthy sacrifice, Nachiketas considered offering himself, and finally asked, "To which god would thou offer me?" When his father did not answer, Nachiketas asked a second and third time. Then Vajasravasa answered angrily, "I would give you to death!"

Nachiketas thought to himself, "Well, I would not be the first or only one that must face death. Like every other man, I will die sooner or later, so why not face death now?" So Nachiketas traveled to the abode of death, where dwelled a god called Yama. Upon arrival, he was told that Yama was away on his travels. Determined to meet death, Nachiketas waited outside for three days without food. When Yama finally returned home, his servants informed him that a Brahmin (they assumed Nachiketas was a member of the Hindu caste of priests because of his spiritual maturity) had waited three days to see him "burning like the spirit of fire." They urged Yama to soothe him with an offering of water, for one who refuses hospitality to a Brahmin betrays God. Impressed with this stranger's sincerity, Yama agreed to speak with Nachiketas, and said, "Since you have come here as a sacred guest, without hospitality for three days and three nights, you may choose any three wishes and I will grant them."

Nachiketas' first wish was simple. He asked, "May my father's anger be appeased so I will be remembered and welcomed when I return home." Yama readily granted his wish, adding that his father would be overjoyed on discovering his son had escaped an encounter with death.

The next wish Nachiketas asked for was more complex. Noting that Heaven was free of hunger, thirst, old age, and even death, he asked Yama to explain to him the sacred fire that leads there. Yama told him about the fire of creation. It was, he said, the beginning of all worlds and the basis of the fire sacrifice, which was explained and would from now on be called by his name. Yama further explained that one who lights the fire three times, attains union with the Three, and performs three holy actions, would know the god of fire and pass beyond the bonds of life and death to find supreme peace in Heaven.

Finally, instructed by Death to make his third wish, Nachiketas replied, "Oh, Yama, god of death, tell me what happens to a man after death? Does he survive? Please reveal this greatest mystery to me." Stunned, Yama begged Nachiketas to ask another question, offering instead vast wealth, power and fame, beautiful women, long-lived children and grandchildren, personal longevity, or anything else a mortal could ever want... anything but the secrets of death. But Natchiketas knew that all these things were transient and refused, asking Yama instead to keep his promise.

Yama saw that Nachiketas was both sincere and firm. He then became most serious and replied, "Nachiketas, tempted not by worldly things, you are man of wisdom. Now I will explain the secrets of death. Two paths exist in life, the path of joy and the path of pleasure. The wise man follows the former while the fool follows the latter. Those who believe the worldly life is the only one will go from death to death. The eternal is not reached through the transitory, nor is sacred knowledge attained by logic or reason. The wise man, contemplating the God who dwells both in the heart as Atman and in the mystery of things as Brahman, transcends pleasure and sorrow, and finds joy in the supreme Self, the source of all joy. He leaves the world of sorrow and delusion behind." Then Yama made the following analogy, "The body is but a chariot, Atman is its Lord, and reason the driver. The horses pulling the chariot are a man's senses and the paths they follow are the objects of his desire. He who has right understanding has control of the chariot. He who lets his horses run wild, who chases pleasure only, will wander from death to death. When a man's consciousness is one with Atman, when all desires leave his heart, he becomes Brahman and is free of death."

Finally, Yama talked of God. "That consciousness by which all things are known, which is beyond waking, thinking, and dreaming, which is never born and never dies, animating all life and resting in every thing that is, that in which the sun rises and sets and even the gods are born, that one Spirit is God. He who perceives the one behind the many never dies. He is the sun, the wind, and the sky, the priest *at the altar, the wine in the jar. Untouched by any earthly happenings is the omnipresent consciousness of God, the pure consciousness of all conscious beings. When the mind and senses are still, then He alone is."*

And so Yama taught Nachiketas the secrets of death and eternal life, whereafter his consciousness became one with Brahman and he reached immortality. So indeed will anyone who knows the Atman dwelling in the heart as his greater Self.

Interpretation

From the world's oldest religion, this story is classic Hinduism. It begins with an aging cowherder wishing to enter Heaven who clearly has the wrong idea: you cannot buy or trick your way there. Pure of heart and sincerely wishing to help his father, Natchiketas generously offers himself as a sacrifice to God, but his father bitterly refuses and threatens instead to offer his son to Death.

The first mysterious symbol in this tale is the number three: three questions to the father, three days' wait, three wishes, lighting the fire three times, attaining union with the Three, and three holy actions. It's as if the number three must be fully appreciated before the tale can even proceed. What is the symbolic significance of three?

In mythic creation stories, the one of unity (only God exists) creates the two of duality (God and man, self and other, good and evil, spirit and matter, Heaven and Earth), giving rise to the multiplicity of ordinary life (the "ten thousand things"). The number three is associated with the solution to the problem of duality, a solution requiring the integration of opposites returning us once again to unity (a process Carl Jung called the "transcendent function"). Similarly, in fairy tales, something often must happen three times before a genuinely new development breaks the tension of opposites ("three times a charm"). The number three, therefore, symbolizes the step that resolves a problem arising from the illusions of duality. "Union with the Three" further implies giving oneself over entirely to this task, an act of faith and surrender that ultimately leads to transformation.

The fire ritual, the next mysterious symbol, represents the powers of creation and transformation. The cosmos was born in the fire of the "Big Bang" and we have all used controlled fire to transform things (for example, cook food, power automobiles, release energy's beauty in fireworks). Alchemists viewed fire as a means of transmuting base metal into gold and Jung hypothesized that their theory symbolized the desire to turn unrefined human nature into the purity of divinity, an important insight for this story. Third, many religions describe the bodily heat associated with mystical experiences - yet another sign of transformation.

Sensing Yama's answer is still insufficient, Nachiketas rephrases his question about the mystery of death a third and final time. The question is so profound that Yama tries to dissuade Nachiketas from pursuing it. Why would Yama keep the secret of death from humanity? Mystics and spiritual teachers have long kept secrets, though generally not for selfish reasons. Spiritual knowledge is withheld because novice seekers are not capable of understanding it and the titillation of amazing ideas would only become a distraction from their spiritual practice. Secrecy also exists because the general population often ridicules esoteric knowledge, making it appear foolish or impossible. Yama is not so much about keeping secrets as protecting them for those who are spiritually ready.

When all manner of bribery fails, Yama realizes that this boy has already transcended his attachment to worldly things, a test that must be passed by every realized being (Jesus and Buddha were both offered worldly temptations in futile attempts to lure them off the path of enlightenment). Now Death begins to divulge his secrets, expounding an esoteric knowledge that is the essence of both Hinduism and universal mystical teachings.

There are two paths in the world, Yama explains. The path of pleasure corresponds to the ego's pursuit of worldly gratifications – wealth, fame, power, and self-importance, a journey that inevitably leads to attachment, addiction, suffering and loss. A man on this path loses control of his life and does not even know it. The path of joy, Yama continues, emanates from union with God as the supreme Self and divine ground of all being.

Yama then talks directly of God. He explains that what man takes to be his own consciousness is actually divine consciousness, but to know this consciousness, one must surrender the fantasy of a personal self, the one imagined to be thinking, doing and dreaming. Made entirely of thought and imagination, this false self idea dissolves naturally and spontaneously in the thought-free consciousness that is divinity, and when thought ceases, so does the identity it creates – until we start thinking again.

Experiencing divine consciousness then reveals the secret of the fire sacrifice and death itself: when pure consciousness focuses on the subjective experience of one's physical being, duality dissolves into unity, solving the problem of three. Instead of the duality of consciousness and being, there is simply conscious being. In the process, we discover the "mystery of Braham" in all things, for everything is made of divinity. In this natural experience of divine union, the seeker finds pure joy, described by the ancient Hindu equation sat-chit-ananda: existence-consciousness-bliss. It is all one and we are that. The seeker has released his belief in identity and, through conscious being, become one with God.

How do we apply Yama's esoteric teachings to the transformation of consciousness associated with aging? The realities of loss and death in the aging process invite us to surrender not only worldly pleasures, possessions, and beliefs, but the whole fictional story of self – our own personal fairy tale. In its purest form, enlightenment describes a consciousness freed from the illusion of individuality and sourced from divinity. The Elder who has relinquished personal identity is especially equipped to step into this unity. This is the deepest transformation of aging. Joseph Campbell, the great mythologist, described it this way,

> *The problem in middle life, when the body has reached its climax of power and begins to decline, is to identify yourself not with the body, which is falling away, but with consciousness of which it is a vehicle. This is something I learned from myths. Am I the bulb that carries the light, or am I the light of which the bulb is a vehicle?... But the body is a vehicle of consciousness, and if you can identify with the consciousness, you can watch this body go like an old car. There goes the fender, there goes the tire, one thing after another – but it's predictable. And then, gradually, the whole thing drops off, and consciousness rejoins consciousness.*

Conclusions

In the western mindset, few can conceive of a life not centered in the construct of the separate ego. From birth to death, it's all about the story of "me." As we saw with both King O'Toole and Inanna, however, the day arrives when we are challenged to surrender the identity, achievements and possessions of the individual self, unconditionally and without guarantee, to something else, something greater, a surrender often symbolized by the specter of death. Despite his maturity and goodness, King O'Toole was completely unprepared to meet God and Death; perhaps that is why he did not learn Death's secrets. Love led Inanna into the shattering ambush of her own death; like me, she, too, was utterly unprepared. With the prescience of the spiritually precocious, however, Nachiketas understands the importance of preparation and chooses to confront Death directly to learn his lessons and help his aging father.

Until now, only a handful of seekers have understood

Nachiketas' realization of divine consciousness, but many teachers now report that the frequency of such enlightenment is increasing, and the new longevity of aging offers this possibility to all of us. Like Nachiketas, we, too, may discover that the self-idea has masked a much greater consciousness and that unity is found in rejoining consciousness and being – the original duality that created the manifest world.

We are each going to die and the project of self is going to fail – these inevitabilities erode the false security of the fictional self. But if we take this process seriously, it may also offer us a chance to experience enlightenment in this lifetime. What if aging invites us to progressively dissolve the fairy tale of self into the pure consciousness that is divinity, and then dissolve duality in the merging of consciousness and being? We cannot know what this is like until we do it, but then we see the other path Death pointed out to Natchiketas. To whatever extent we experience and integrate this unity experience into our lives, to that extent we will contribute to transforming the world.

Reflections

I have been watching the fenders and tires of my bodily car fall off ever more frequently in recent years. Elevated cholesterol and triglycerides, heart arrhythmia, bone marrow abnormalities, rotator cuff tears, diminished energy…I would love a miraculous "tune-up!" Things are indeed breaking down on me, but as King O'Toole demonstrated, turning to the soul for new inspiration has been a boon. I am re-inspired and excited about the new journey of age. But now Death also seems to be telling me that there is yet another great discovery to be made in this process: when everything we are falls away, what's left is the consciousness of divinity.

While consciousness has always been with us, we rarely take time to examine it. We have instead focused on its ever-changing contents – ideas, worries, goals, beliefs, memories, fantasies and the endless sensations and perceptions of everyday life. But when I stop thinking for a moment and focus on the resulting thought-free awareness, it feels as if I have opened a door to eternity. I know this must sound strange but it's the best way I can describe it. In that space, I sense the ultimate consciousness that is the mother of all things, including "me." Moreover, this consciousness seems to be everywhere, residing in all things. In fact, from this perspective, it is the essence of all things. That consciousness, Death explains, belongs not to me but to the universe. Called Cosmic Consciousness, Buddha-mind, Christ Consciousness, Presence, Brahman, God, and a thousand other names, it is the divine consciousness saturating reality, the consciousness that we mistakenly believe is our own. Dwelling in this non-personal consciousness shifts the felt center of my being from the construct of "me" to something vastly largely.

The world I experience changes radically in this consciousness. If "I" am not that important than neither are "my" problems. No self, no problem! And from this open space, behavior flows in a new and casual way – things just happen, for there is no one to direct them. Instead of swimming up stream pursing the ego's goals, I relax and float effortlessly down stream. This is the change of life that can come with aging. Surrendering self and its demands, the world becomes a divine mystery once again. Aging has brought me into a consciousness that transforms everything!

Your Story

Reflecting on your own story...

Most of us fear dying and don't even want to talk about it. Nachiketas, on the other hand, goes to meet Death directly and is rewarded for his courage and tenacity. What questions would you like to ask Death? Write a dialogue with Death. Let it flow spontaneously without planning and see where it takes you. When you make peace with Death, your fear of dying may diminish substantially.

Have you noticed moments in your aging experience when thought seems to stop by itself and you seem to wake up as if from a dream? Perhaps you are sitting quietly outside on the deck and suddenly become aware of the world around you. This is a moment of heightened consciousness where you shift from the path of ego gratification to the path of awakening. What happened in that moment?

What do you notice when you intentionally stop thinking and focus awareness on consciousness itself? Describe this experience in as much detail as possible. What happens when you focus this thought-free consciousness on the physical sensation of your own being? These two steps are central to the mystical experience and part of all great spiritual paths. How are they part of your own spiritual practice? How might you focus on them more?

Fetch Me a Cup of Water

The Power of Enchantment

Despite its profundity, our discovery of the ultimate significance of consciousness can be lost and forgotten in a heartbeat. This next oft-told tale from the Eastern spiritual traditions illustrates how easily fantasy and illusion repossess the awareness of even the most determined seeker. Its popularity is evident in the fact that sometimes the teacher in this story is Krishna, other times, Buddha.

Narada, whose name means wisdom giver, was a famous devotee of the god Vishnu. He journeyed to visit Lord Krishna to ask him to explain maya, the cause of the world's illusions.

Narada and Krishna went out for a walk. Narada said, "The great sages tell of maya, the power by which you make the whole universe appear to be what it is not, deluding us into ideas of you and me, this and that, now and then, and the multiplicity of things, when all is one unity. What is this power of maya? Will you reveal its secrets to me?"

"I will happily fulfill your desire," Krishna replied as Narada and Krishna continued their stroll. After walking a very long distance, Krishna became quite thirsty, and said, "Narada, I am thirsty. We cannot return home to quench my thirst. Can you get me a cup of water from the village up ahead? I will sit here until you return."

"Your wish is my command, Lord Krishna."

Filled with the desire to be of service to this incarnation of Vishnu, Narada hurried on to the village. He reached the first house and knocked on the door, which was opened by a young girl whose radiant beauty immediately enchanted him. Instantly he forgot all about Krishna and his request for water and instead fell head over heels in love. Narada asked, "Who are you and who is your father? I would be most fortunate and blessed if I might marry you."

"My father is inside. Come in," she said, whereupon Narada met and discussed marriage with the young woman's father.

"Sir, my name is Narada. I am Krishna's devoted servant. I have fallen in love with your daughter and wish to marry her. It would be the grace of Brahman if you consented." Her father readily accepted Narada's proposal.

The wedding took place in a matter of days. Over the next twelve years, Narada's wife bore him several children and great happiness filled his family life.

One day, however, the sky grew unusually dark, rain clouds mounted, the winds howled furiously and thunderclaps shook the landscape. Soon the village was flooded and many ran to escape the rising waters. Narada collected his most precious belongings, held hands with his wife and children, carried the youngest children on his shoulders, and waded into the swift current. The swirling waters soon took all his belongings and he cried out for his lost wealth. The waters then took his beloved oldest son and then, one by one, the rest of his children. Narada's suffering grew nearly unbearable. He clung desperately to his wife and cried out, "Why have you forsaken me, Krishna? Why do you not protect your faithful servant?" Suddenly a huge wave tore his wife from him. In that moment, life became hopeless and meaningless.

As if in response to Narada's final anguished cry, an immense flash of lightning lit up the dark sky momentarily blinding his eyes. When he opened them again, he was stunned by what lay before him. Or more correctly, what didn't. The storm, the devastation, his family, and the village were utterly and completely gone, replaced by the visage of Krishna, sitting quietly beneath a tree, looking at him.

"Narada, I have been awaiting your return for almost half an hour. Have you brought me the water I requested?" A mischievous smile began to play on Krishna's face.

Suddenly Narada understood everything. He rushed to Krishna, bowed low, and wept like a child. "Today," Narada said, "you showed me the power of maya and I was completely deluded. The maya of self, *family and everyday life made me confuse the impermanent world of desire with the joy and release of transcendence. Pursuing illusions, I lost you and wandered instead in a delirium of fantasy. Please, Krishna, may I never be so affected again."*

Without hesitation, and filled with love, Krishna granted Narada's wish and touched him gently, whereupon Narada found himself in the highest realms of Heaven.

Interpretation

Maya, a Sanskrit word, is a central idea in Eastern religious traditions. The root ma means "not" and ya translates loosely to "that." This definition is meant to imply that things are not what they seem. Rather, the mind, with its constant thought, imagination, and fantasy, colors and distorts all we see, projecting itself on reality like a movie film. This is maya and it creates all the illusions that drive our busy and often distressing world.

Narada asks Krishna how maya functions, and his request is granted sooner and more powerfully than he ever expected. He was shown how quickly and easily his consciousness could be completely hijacked by the illusions of fantasy – literally instantly! – illusions that held him in a dream-like state for years. All it takes is a pretty girl, new ambition, careless driver, nasty comment, worried thought or screaming child, and our thought-free conscious is taken over by an imagined emotional drama. Indeed, the simple idea of self seems to generate endless scenarios to worry about. This is the path of pleasure and pain that Yama described to Natchiketas. It's not that events don't happen, it's not that love, marriage, children and career are wrong, it's that we project so much additional meaning onto them – fantasies of fulfillment, feelings of inferiority, fears of failure or dreams of fame.

When we learn to see the world in a consciousness free of thought, we quickly discover that it is not what we imagine. Some argue that our whole life is a dream manufactured and projected from inside – the light of divinity passing through an internal film of stored ideas, images and symbols to create the movie of our lives, something like what the Elder-Tree Mother showed the boy in our first story. Whether you believe this or not, it is enough to observe how much of everyday life does in fact conform to this process. As we project soap opera fantasies onto reality – "Does he love me?" "Will I be famous?" "Am I in trouble?" – we create a perpetual self-made drama. What would it mean to wake up from this dream?

Many spiritual practices like meditation, mindfulness and mystical consciousness give us tools to do just this. The experience of aging provides yet another path for waking up. As consciousness empties of thought, belief, and fantasy with age, we begin to see through the illusions that drove our lives for so many years. We ask ourselves questions like, "Was success really that important?" "Did my looks matter that much?" "How big a house did I really need?" "Who cares what others think about me?" As we used to say, "It's all in your head!" and it is. As they wake up from the dream of life, enlightened Elders begin to question maya everywhere.

When Narada wakes up from his dream, he immediately resolves to take Yama's second path – the joy of transcendence. Released from the chains of illusion, he is ecstatic. As the story suggests, this path leads directly to Heaven, though Heaven is most accurately defined as the experience of divinity every-where. With this definition, Heaven need not only be in the next world, for we may also find it here. And for the enlightened Elder, it is the ultimate destination of aging, as we will see in our next tale.

Reflections

I watch this process of maya arise in myself all the time. One moment I am present and happily dwelling in consciousness, letting things be as they are, and then, without even noticing, my consciousness is taken over by a worry or concern: "Do we have enough money to pay this bill?" "Is so-and-so mad at me?" "I miss my children and grandchildren." Then, I am no longer "here and now," I am "there and then," lost in fantasy. The good news is that I wake up sooner now, for I more quickly recognize when I have fallen back into daydreaming again. How? The most immediate reminder is the presence of emotional distress. In consciousness, there is freedom, wonder, joy and love; when consciousness is clouded by the mind's beliefs and fantasies, I find myself feeling upset, anxious, excited, angry or sad.

One of the great boons of aging for me has been the recognition that I am the source of my distress. Years ago I went on a vision quest in the desert – three days of preparation with a small group of seekers, three days alone in the wilderness with only water, and three days to share our experience and prepare to re-enter the world. Though virtually nothing of significance changed around me each day I was alone, I watched myself cycle through countless feelings and fantasies. They all came from me. So it is with everyday life. Age and experience have taught me that distress means maya; it is a great motivator to wake up.

Your Story

Reflecting on your own story…

What event, circumstance or fantasy took you into maya today? Can you remember dramas or fantasies that possessed your consciousness for years, like a hurtful relationship, domineering boss, or a career ambition? How and when did you wake up from them?

What are your most seductive fantasies or illusions, the ones that still hijack your awareness? One of the gifts of aging is recognizing these fantasies, and questioning them sooner. Having been tricked hundreds of times, we finally begin to see the hook.

How do you know when you have fallen back into the dream

world again? Do you have a practice or method for waking up when this happens? If not, see if you can learn one, such as observing the operation of your thoughts and fantasies in meditation.

The Lady and the Fountain

The Discovery of Heaven on Earth

This rather long tale, from the King Arthur legends of twelfth and thirteenth century Europe, brings us back to the Tree of Life in a most powerful and dramatic way. A complex and rich saga of quest, betrayal, forgetting and returning, it is retold here in abbreviated form to emphasize the details most relevant to the journey of awakening. Although this story is not strictly about aging, it describes the same profound shift from middle-aged doing to the peaceful unity of conscious being found in aging. To understand this tale is to understand the dynamics of the Elder's journey from the illusions of maya to the divine world.

On one of those rare days when King Arthur and the Knights of the Round Table were between adventures, they were sitting in chamber drinking mead and telling stories, whereupon the king fell asleep and a young knight told a most peculiar tale.

On a recent journey to a strange and distant land, a most remarkable experience had taken place. On the summit of a hill, in an open space, in front of a huge and majestic tree, the knight came upon a natural fountain pouring forth from a rock ledge. Next to the fountain was a silver bowl attached by a silver chain to a marble slap. With the bowl, he poured water onto the slab whereupon the sky instantly darkened and a tremendous shower of hail fell upon the knight and his horse, devastating everything in sight. The downpour would have killed the knight and his steed had he not used his shield for protection. When the hail ended, every leaf on the tree was gone but the sky cleared and vast flocks of colorful birds filled the tree with unequaled song. Then, just as suddenly, the youth found himself confronting a ferocious Black Knight charging toward him upon a powerful black stallion. After several passes, the intruder's lance cut the reins of the younger man's horse and he takes it, forcing the defeated knight to wend his way back to Camelot on foot.

Now listening to this tale was a knight named Owain and it touched his soul so deeply that he resolved to leave the very next day to find this magical fountain. With only rough directions, he rode for many days through mountain and valley until at last he arrived at a distant land. There he was welcomed by the lord of a large castle, the Castle of Abundance, who offered him a bath, clean clothes, a feast and beautiful handmaidens to attend his every need. Though invited to remain as long as he wished, Owain resumed his search the very next day following directions offered by the lord of the castle. Then, deep in a wilderness, Owain came upon a monstrous black figure with one leg and one eye, surrounded by dragons and serpents. Unafraid, he walked directly up to the giant and asked for directions to the magic fountain. The giant, recognizing Owain's fearlessness, simply pointed the way.

Owain finally reached the magic fountain and, as the younger knight had, poured water onto the rock slab. As before, the sky darkened instantly, hail bombarded the countryside, Owain saved himself and his steed beneath his shield, and the storm passed just as suddenly leaving the leafless tree filled with the most melodious birds. But Owain also knew the Black Knight would come next and indeed he did. The most ferocious battled ensued, ending only when Owain struck his attacker a piercing blow to the head. Mortally wounded, the Black Knight fled to a castle where he disappeared behind a gate. As Owain pursued him through the gate, the great portcullis fell sharply on his horse directly behind the saddle cutting the steed in half and knocking off his spurs. Owain now found himself trapped between two gates in mortal danger. Through a small visor in the inner door, however, he spied a young maiden with yellow hair and dress. The maiden, whose name was Luned, offered him a magic ring that would render him invisible to the guards now opening the inner gate. She then told Owain where to meet her upon his escape.

Owain found Luned where she promised to be waiting. Arriving at *her abode, Owain was given drink and food in gold and silver bowls. That night Owain and Luned heard that the nobleman who owned this castle was dead. A great funeral took place the next day during which Owain saw that the dead nobleman was in fact the Black Knight he had slain. By his side a beautiful woman wailed with the most intense grief. This woman, the maiden explained, was the Black Knight's wife, the Countess of the Fountain. Owain immediately fell in love with her. He then learned the remarkable law of the castle: whoever slew the Black Knight became the next Black Knight. He learned also that Luned was the Countess' handmaiden who promised to intercede on his behalf.*

When Owain fell asleep, Luned went to the Countess of the Fountain and, in keeping the timeless law of the castle, convinced her that the castle would go undefended unless she remarried. Deceitfully, Luned proposed to travel to Camelot in search of a suitable knight from King Arthur's Round Table. The Countess reluctantly agreed to this plan. After enough time passed, Luned brought Owain to the Countess, who immediately spotted the deception, for Owain did not appear as one who had traveled for days. Her intuition also told her his true identity as slayer of her husband. Still, the Countess knew the law and needed a new guardian to protect her kingdom. And so Owain and the Countess married, Owain became the Black Knight, and together they lived in the rapt joy of this enchanted land.

Back in Camelot, however, King Arthur and his knights had grown increasingly concerned for Owain's safety and whereabouts. Planning to be gone only three weeks, Owain was now missing three years! A search party was assembled, and guessing that he had gone in search of the legendary fountain, the king and his men followed the same route past the Kingdom of Abundance and the terrifying monster, finally arriving at the fountain. Pouring a bowl of water on the slab, they endured the terrible storm, the melodious birds, and came face to face the Black Knight. Concealed by their armor, neither side recognized the other until Owain, in the midst of mighty combat, knocked the visor from his old friend Gawain's helmet and recognized him immediately. A great reunion then took place between these long separated comrades and Owain invited King Arthur and his men to the castle. There a banquet lasted three months.

When it was time for King Arthur to return home, he beseeched the Countess of the Fountain to allow Owain to return as well. Reluctantly she gave her permission, due only to the great respect she had for this legendary king, and Owain journeyed back to Camelot to complete his duties. His return was to be for three months only, but something else happened. Owain became so involved with his old life of pomp and chivalry that he forgot entirely about his place as the Black Knight. Then one day, an old hag dressed in yellow rode her horse right into King Arthur's chambers directly up to Owain, accused him with the worst betrayal, demanded the return of Luned's ring, and left with it.

Shattered with the violent grief of his terrible forgetting, Owain left Camelot to wander for months in a remote and barren land. There he was reduced nearly to a wild beast by hunger, isolation, and the unforgiving landscape. Nearly dead, Owain stumbled into the land of a widowed countess and collapsed. There he was found by the countess and her maidens and a potent balm rubbed on his chest above his heart. With a fresh horse and new clothes, healed from his near fatal malaise but still lost and confused, Owain wandered off again through the wilderness. Soon he came upon a terrific battle between a serpent and a black lion. Slaying the dragon won him instant loyalty from the lion, and they became great friends traveling together all over this remote and harsh landscape leaving a trail of legendary adventures of the Knight and the Lion.

Unknown to Owain, Luned had also been exiled to this same land for bringing her Countess a husband who betrayed her. As punishment, Luned was imprisoned in a dungeon awaiting execution unless the Black Knight should rescue her. And indeed he did. After days of travel, our knight and his lion came again upon the monster of the forest, who tricked Owain into locking up the lion so they might have a fair fight. Fortunately the lion escaped and slew the monster.

Owain and the lion also slew the henchmen sent to execute Luned and all three resolved to return to the Countess of the Fountain. Luned reconciled with her queen who had not recognized Owain. She begged this fine knight and his lion to stay on but he would not tarry, nor did he reveal his identity. Under his breath, Owain whispered that she alone held the casket in which his happiness was locked and buried. Then, bidding Luned good-bye, he left with the lion, but not before begging Luned to speak well of the former Black Knight to the Countess.

One day Owain and the lion arrived back at the magic fountain by the tree. Repeating the ritual and the storm, Owain waited but no Black Knight came to protect the fountain or its kingdom. Meanwhile, back in the kingdom, Luned was convincing the Countess that the Knight and his Lion would be good defenders of the realm. When the Countess finally agreed, Luned fetched the knight. Though she was at first furious at Owain upon discovering his true identity, he begged her love and forgiveness, and she soon acquiesced to his heartfelt sincerity. The Black Knight and the Countess of the Fountain were reconciled.

Finally, after a season of bliss, the Countess told her husband she would happily accompany him to Camelot if he so wished. She explained that there she will be visible only to him, so that he might have both worlds in one. Owain wondered what would become of her kingdom and the Countess reassured him that she and her kingdom were one and that it went wherever she did. And so the tale of the Lady and the Fountain ends.

Interpretation

Our story begins during a lull in King Arthur's normally exciting and quest-driven Court – an exceptionally masculine version of Yama's first path. The king falls asleep, implying that the usual and customary rules of the court can be temporarily relaxed to let in another kind of consciousness, one associated with reverie, fairy tale, and imagination. From this opening into the collective unconscious springs a phantasmal dream world where anything can happen, the secrets of the spiritual journey are revealed, and a different kind of adventure emerges – the adventure of awakening.

A young knight describes his experience in a strange and distant land. The description of this incredible place – a flowing fountain atop a hill, in an open space, before a huge tree – strongly suggests that he has stumbled upon a sacred and powerful site reminiscent of the Tree of Life in the Garden of Eden, an awesome and other-worldly place. The pouring of sacred water on a marble slab represents the alchemical act of bringing spirit to substance or, for the mystic, consciousness to being, triggering a violent downpour of hail, a sign that great cosmic energies have been unleashed. The young knight is ill-prepared for such immense spiritual power. Fortunately his shield saves him, signifying that his hard-won masculine strength and courage, or perhaps the power of the sacred emblem or words on it, has protected him. The birds' celestial song suggests the re-stabilizing of sacred energies. In sum, this young and naive knight tampered with the place where divinity flows into Creation – a common symbol for the Garden of Eden, nearly costing him his life.

Our protagonist, Owain, symbolizes that rare intuitive individual (or that rare consciousness in each of us) who immediately recognizes the profound possibility of experiencing the divine in this world, and must, driven by this same realization, initiate a sacred quest to reach it. Without hesitation, he travels far and wide, resisting the temptation to settle for a life of wealth, ease, and instant gratification offered by the Lord of Abundance (or modern advertising!). Owain is equally unafraid of the monstrous threshold guardian that would frighten lesser men, symbolizing the fear of death that must be faced by those seeking enlightenment. Interestingly, this particular guardian, with his single eye and leg, secretly symbolizes – and presages – the unity consciousness associated with spiritual awakening.

Our hero eventually finds the sacred fountain in the mysterious garden. Unlike his immature young predecessor, Owain is prepared to fight the Black Knight and, in fact, defeats him, a testimony to the importance of preparation and unyielding courage on the spiritual journey. Pursuing the mortally wounded Black Knight, however, Owain suddenly finds himself trapped between two gates with his stead cut in half. Symbolically speaking, Owain is now caught between the two worlds (variously characterized as the profane and the sacred, or the World and Man and Heaven on Earth) and cannot resort to the powerful physical strength that brought him here, represented by the horse. With his masculine resources completely paralyzed, the feminine now makes her first appearance.

Luned represents the consciousness of the anima replacing the masculine, goal-oriented male ego. Named after the moon and symbolizing the supernatural realm of night, mystery, and dreams, Luned brings Owain a magic ring that makes him invisible, that is, erases all outward signs of personal identity and existence, exactly what enlightened consciousness does in dissolving the self-idea. Owain has just experienced a taste of that transformation.

Luned invites Owain into her abode, that is, into the feminine mode of consciousness, where he is served from sacred dishes and learns the shocking law of this enchanted land, a version of the karmic principle popularly translated as "what goes around comes around." Thus, whoever kills the Black Knight must take his place. This law also suggests that the Countess and her sacred fountain require a mature and powerful masculine presence, a boundary-maker, to protect them from profane intrusion or desecration. Whoever defeats this guardian must bear full responsibility and take his place. Moreover, we see that the energies of the archetypal feminine and masculine modes of consciousness must be in balance for the Garden to prosper. So, enchanted by the sacred feminine, Owain falls in love with the Countess and expects to serve as the Black Knight.

Sometimes the ways of the inner feminine are clever, as when matchmakers manipulate – in the name of love – a particular man and woman to meet, and so Luned brings Owain and the Countess together. Despite the heart-wrenching circumstances of their initial encounter, the Countess overcomes her personal grief in surrender to the higher purpose of this land: the original duality of Adam and Eve, each fulfilling his or her purpose in the Garden. The archetypal balance of the sacred is restored: Divinity giving life and purpose to its complementary halves, man and woman, who now serve and protect the sacred fountain flowing into Paradise.

The enchanted land of the sacred fountain – Heaven on Earth – knows nothing of time, for enlightenment is outside of time, but in dualistic Camelot, time is a standard measure of reality, and too much time has passed for King Arthur to ignore. And so the King and his men, with the same requisite preparation and courage, seek their lost comrade and reunite in great celebration. Unbeknownst to them, the two separate worlds – unity and duality – are now destined to collide producing yet another profound disruption of Owain's state of consciousness. This cataclysm is set in motion when Owain is given permission to return to Camelot for a visit.

Returning to the dualistic world of King Arthur's Court, Owain loses touch with Garden consciousness and then forgets it altogether, a forgetting that happens all the time in our lives – the maya that Krishna revealed to Narada. How many times have we felt the holy, come into its Presence, stepped into Paradise, only to lose it entirely with the next worried thought, grand plan, or emotional upset? But for Owain, who has come to know the goddess intimately and lived in the timeless mystical consciousness of Heaven on Earth, facing a loss of this magnitude will be crushing. And so one day the Countess, representing the inner shape-shifting feminine made old and angry by years of insensitivity and neglect, confronts Owain with his betrayal and takes back Luned's magical ring, the symbol of their unity. Put differently, Owain suddenly realizes that he has betrayed his own soul – the feminine side of himself, and his earlier experience of enlightenment.

Owain falls into a profound depression characterized by excruciating feelings of desolation, disorientation, and self-recrimination. Unremitting and unforgiving, Owain's self-hatred nearly kills him, but once again, powerless to help himself, the feminine consciousness intervenes. Another version of the abandoned feminine, the widowed countess brings him back to life by restoring his heart, that is, his capacity to love.

Despite his healing, Owain continues to wander lost and confused, for he has yet to reconcile with the Countess, his abandoned feminine side. Along the way, Owain slays an awesome snake, symbolizing mastery of the life force (which King O'Toole's goose, a lesser being, could not vanquish in our first story), and teams up with a lion, symbolizing the restoration of a healthy physical masculinity. Such tests and trials are fundamental to the spiritual journey and critical for seeker's maturity and preparation for enlightenment. Thereafter, inspired by higher values, the duo perform many good deeds biding their time until the ultimate reconciliation can occur.

What does Luned's exile mean? As a consequence of his self-hatred, Owain exiled part of his own inner feminine. Seeking healing and redemption, he saves Luned by killing the henchmen of the self-hatred imprisoning her in his psyche. As a consequence, Luned reconciles with the Countess, resolving the split in the feminine archetype, for the feminine can also turn on itself. Amazingly Owain still refuses to reveal his true identity to the Countess; instead he moves on, for the inner work on himself remains unfinished.

Finally and inexorably drawn back to the fountain, Owain,

like all spiritual seekers, returns to the divine source. He discovers that the position of Black Knight remains unfilled – his work is still unfinished. With the healing of the feminine, the Countess finally understands the deep and sacred value of reconciling with Owain, though she still had to overcome remnants of her wounded heart and pride. Witnessing Owain's heartfelt sincerity, the Countess softens and their love restores the archetypal order of the divine world. It is a time of bliss and fulfillment in the consciousness of Heaven on Earth.

As the Countess, Owain's feminine side, learns that he is trustworthy, she makes peace with her old betrayal wound and agrees to accompany him back into the dualistic world of King Arthur's Court. The only catch is that no one else will be able to see her, symbolizing the invisibility of sacred feminine consciousness in the materialistic World of Man. For Owain, however, this condition means that he now lives in both worlds, for whenever he brings his awareness to her invisible presence, their Garden returns.

Conclusions

The Lady and the Fountain describes the questing ego in search of the divine world. As the central protagonist, Owain represents each of us, the collective Everyman, who must devote himself to the pursuit of awakened consciousness so that the sacred marriage of masculine and feminine, consciousness and being, Heaven and Earth, can occur. The purpose of this union, which enlightened Elders will bring to humanity, is no less then the next stage of human spiritual evolution integrating a new Heaven and new Earth into one.

King Arthur, his knights, and the land of Camelot represent the present masculine world of problems, goals and conquests, which we must leave to find the sacred. This masculine side of the personality embodies our heroic, forceful, questing and confronting energies. While responsible for so much cultural and scientific progress, it has also become too one-sided in our day and age, tipping the balance toward compulsive competition, horrific aggression, and the exploitation of the Earth and her resources. As Inanna taught us, it has also driven the divine feminine underground. The women in the story – the Countess, Luned, the widowed countess, and various handmaidens – are all aspects of the feminine side of the personality that can be loving, present-centered, care-taking, intuitive, and generative in its higher forms, but also angry, vengeful, deceitful and punitive in its less mature forms. Ultimately the Black Knight and the Countess symbolize the archetypal caretakers of the sacred fountain – Adam and Eve – whose sacred marriage brings divinity into the world.

The countess symbolizes Mother Earth, Creation, and the divine feminine. The Black Knight symbolizes the ego's attainment of enlightened consciousness. As the Taoist yang and yin symbol balances the opposites of black and white, the knight is black to balance with the white of the goddess, but neither color should be considered ultimately good or bad, better or worse, for such judgments reflect the dualistic consciousness that cannot see Heaven on Earth. Like indigenous rituals in which individuals dress and act like animals or supernatural beings in order to experience their power or wisdom, Owain must put on the costume of the Black Knight to experience – and then embody – his consciousness and purpose.

In the marriage of masculine and feminine sides of himself, Owain transcends his separative ego and merges consciousness with being, whereby divinity is known to be everything and everywhere, as Natchiketas learned. Thus, by dissolving this duality, he also dissolves the split between Heaven and Earth, yielding the experience of Heaven on Earth. Owain then lives with the Countess in timeless mystical consciousness of the imminent divine for what would have been three Earth years. But despite this amazing achievement, there is one more even greater challenge on the road to paradise: staying there. Though many have had mystical experiences, rare is the individual mature enough to remain in its purified consciousness – Narada's powerful lesson. Upon returning to the dualistic world with its false selves and thought-generated reality, Owain once again falls under the spell of identity, time, and story, and the secret entrance into the divine world disappears. The tale suggests that the ultimate task of illuminated consciousness is to bring it back into the everyday world. At the end of the story, Owain has become the bodhisattva, the shaman, the realized man, the one who lives in both worlds, balances Heaven and Earth, and opens the divine world to others.

In sum, this ancient story illustrates how difficult and rare it has historically been for even the most brave and determined individuals to find and stay in sacred consciousness. Very few have reached this highest level of realization. The experience of conscious aging, however, will eventually bring a sea of enlightened Elders into the consciousness of Heaven on Earth, changing the world. Indeed, the story would have been quite different if Owain were an enlightened Elder rather than a brave but naive young man. The young sometimes reach Heaven on Earth by heroic means, but only enlightened Elders bring the capacity to stay.

Reflections

This story captures my own spiritual journey in some amazing ways. Though I grew up without religious instruction, I was always fascinated by religious symbols, reports of mystical and near-death experiences, and the far out idea of Heaven on Earth. Looking back, I realized that I had sensed the divine world as a young child, knew its beauty, light, and consciousness, but lost this awareness as I forced myself to adapt to the conventional world around me. Someplace deep inside, however, I knew it was still here, somewhere, I just didn't know how to find my way back. As a result, I can easily imagine being Owain listening to the young knight's tale of this extraordinary, other-worldly land, knowing without a doubt that it was the divine world here on Earth, and feeling absolutely compelled to seek it.

Like Owain, I eventually learned the secret keys to mystical consciousness, this merging of consciousness and being, and rediscovered the magic of Heaven on Earth. And like Owain, I lost it again in the shattering return of repressed surgical memories and the ending of my career. So painful were these experiences that I could barely remember what Heaven felt like, and wandered years searching for the path again. Nothing worked. Nothing felt right. I suffered trial after trial, failure after failure, and knew the excruciating pain of grief and disorientation. It was only the feminine - in myself as Inanna and in the love from my wife, family, and friends – that brought me back home, for there was no heroic solution to my soul-shattering descent. Only compassion, love, and patience could bring me back. Finally, I, too, felt the kundalini-return of my own life force and the resumption of hope and inspiration. The dying of my previous life gradually blossomed into a new consciousness of aging and its purpose.

I believe that finding, losing and then searching for the divine world is a universal human story. For centuries we thought that divinity is somewhere far away, that this world has fallen from grace, and that we are somehow sinners in hands of a judgmental sky god, when in fact, this world is divinity, and we are, too. Humankind, however, is still trapped in a labyrinth of frightening dualistic thoughts and beliefs. Our ideas lead us to misjudge each other, initiate wars, and create the very enemies we fear. It is time to wake up from this destructive dream and experience life directly – as sacred, precious, and perfect. This will be the great work of the enlightened Elder.

Your Story

Reflecting on your own story…

Can you imagine the possibility of experiencing the divine world? Do you dismiss this idea as ridiculous or impossible? How would you feel if you knew beyond a doubt that it was already here and waiting for you to see it? What would you do?

How might The Lady and the Fountain be your story? How and where did you first experience Heaven on Earth (in love, nature, play, creativity, music) and then paid dearly for its loss? How have you been looking for the way back ever since? The poignancy in this story is our own. The conclusion can be our own as well.

Owain spent years in the land of suffering recovering from his failure, burning away karma, and, without realizing it, preparing to meet the goddess of feminine consciousness again. How have you experienced suffering that you later come to see as a time of healing, cleansing, and preparation for enlightenment?

Rahula Eclipses Age

An Elder's Journey To Heaven on Earth

Owain took a lifetime to wake up and find Heaven on Earth. After all, he was stuck in the masculine myth of heroism, bravery, and conquest. What might have happened if he had a spiritual teacher? This twelfth century tale from the Tibetan Buddhist Tantric tradition known as Vajrayana tells of an old man of low caste and little spiritual training who nonetheless achieved enlightenment and paradise far more quickly with the help of an itinerant guru. While the guru's instruction, couched in highly symbolic Buddhist terminology, may seem incomprehensible at first, translating its meaning reveals remarkable wisdom.

Rahula means "He who has grasped Rahu." A terrifying demon from the Hindu tradition, Rahu disguised himself as a god in order to drink the gods' divine nectar and thus acquire their strength and immortality. Before he could swallow it, however, Monini, a female form of the god Vishnu, cut off his head. As a consequence, the head remained immortal. It is said that Rahu's glance is death-inflicting and that he occasionally creates eclipses by swallowing the sun or moon, which then pass out through the open neck to shine again.

Rahula had become an old man unable even to control his basic bodily functions. Despised and abused by family and neighbors, he left home and settled in a cemetery to await death and thereby move onto his next birth. Soon thereafter a yogin, a practitioner of Tantric Buddhism, approached him asking why he was living in a cemetery. Rahula replied, "The moon of my youth has been eclipsed by the Rahu-dragon of old age. My sons and others abuse me, so I remain here, happy to die." The yogin replied, "Your karma is ripening: the rivers of childhood, youth and old age have all flowed past. The river of death has now arrived. Shouldn't you practice the Dharma as provision for death?" With gladness in his heart, Rahula asked to be given the Dharma, the teaching of Buddha that ends mortal suffering.

The yogin explained that the awakened state is free of old age, nor do wealth and poverty, being conditions of mind only, affect this pristine consciousness. The yogin then initiated Rahula, transferring his own spiritual power to the old man, and instructed him to meditate on an image of the moon's circle positioned above the letter A at the top of his head. He was then to picture all the concepts of the world flowing into this circle. The yogin explained, "Eclipse all concepts with the Rahu. When you feel the great bliss at the top of your head, the profound seed-point will arise. By the continuous merging of emptiness and bliss, you will overcome the enemies, the skandhas. The qualities of the Buddhas will arise and lo, there will be unceasing wonders."

The old man experienced the joy of increasing enlightenment and practiced thus for sixteen years, passing on his growing wisdom to others, finally achieving the highest stage of realization. Thereafter he lived for many years in the paradise realm of this world, in the land of divine beings.

Interpretation

In this very symbolic teaching story, our protagonist faces the all-to-common and tragic plight of old age in times past – he is poor, despised, useless, and a burden to others. Beyond hope and preparing to die, he settles in a cemetery, a place symbolizing the reality of death and the futility of samsara – the illusionary world of seeking, wandering, and suffering. At his lowest point, an enlightened teacher arrives (with the timing of St. Kevin!) to offer the healing balm of Buddhist teaching and the transmission of spiritual power flowing down his lineage of awakened teachers.

Rahula metaphorically blames his plight on Rahu, as if this disembodied demon who swallows the sun and moon had swallowed his life. But the yogin sees things differently. He likens

Rahula's life to a series of rivers flowing by – childhood, youth, and old age – bringing him finally to the river of death. His is a fascinating perspective, suggesting perhaps that one can either be in each river's stage of life, or on the banks peacefully watching the stages go by; the former implying an immersion in the samsara illusions of the world, and the latter offering instead a witnessing consciousness free of attachment or identification with these passing stages. These two paths are but another iteration of Yama's teaching to Nathcheketas. The yogin further explains that in this pure consciousness, there can be no old age or any other conditions.

As is the practice in Tantric Buddhism, the yogin then transmits his power to the Rahula through an initation ritual and instructs him on spiritual practice. The story does not describe which initiation is performed but it does illuminate some profound Buddhist practices. Meditating on the moon's circle, a white sphere, is a common beginning Tantric practice. It is a focus on emptiness. Placing this image above the letter "A" may signify its beginning nature or depict a figure practicing this exercise. Visualizing all the concepts of the world entering the empty circle suggests the dissolving of dualistic thought into nothingness, that is, pure consciousness. The bliss at the top of the head refers to the Crown Chakra, the body's highest center of consciousness associated with complete enlightenment and the total dissolution of duality. By combining emptiness and bliss, the concentrated seed point of awakening blossoms into the consciousness that overcomes the skandhas, the mental functions that create maya's illusions of self and world.

As a result of these instructions, Rahula achieves an expanding enlightenment in old age. Rahu, as pure non-dual consciousness, devours the illusions of age and death, freeing Rahula from the imagined torments of physical decline. Rahula continues to practice for many more years, a most fruitful "old age," dwelling in the paradise realm of this world, a land of divine beings and implicit reference to Heaven on Earth.

Conclusions

With a yogin's enlightened teaching, Rahula awakens from his depressing beliefs about aging to a consciousness beyond belief, that in turn reveals the presence of the divine world all around him. The story suggests that the potential spiritual awakening of aging can be accelerated with the right insights, instructions, experiences and practices; Owain might have bypassed a lot of suffering with such teaching. Indeed, the story suggests that old age is a mental illusion, one that breeds sorrow and futility; but transcending thought and illusion, we discover a world beyond our wildest expectations.

Reflections

Like the old man in this story, I felt useless and unwanted in the months and years following my premature retirement, often visiting the cemetery of depression as if waiting to die. Indeed, the idea of me was dying. Did Saint Kevin or a yogin visit me at this lowest of times? Yes, in a way.

The voice that came to me throughout my darkness was always my own, but it was voice not of ego, but of consciousness. It kept saying things like, "This is not what you think. You do not exist. You are not this. You are what I am. You are the consciousness of the universe. Wake up! I am you."

We all have access to this voice for we are all conscious. As the yogin in this story suggested, dissolve concepts and you find the consciousness in which they arise. That consciousness is the Presence we have historically called "God." The mystics have repeatedly told us, "You are that." To wake up means to release all concepts, especially the "I" thought, and dwell in and as consciousness as Self. Then all ideas dissolve, including "you," "time," "age" and "death" and we are free. The Eastern mystics have spoken this message most clearly over the millennia, so it is not surprising that Yama, Krishna and the yogin all repeat it in their effort to awaken us. We are as close to enlightenment as consciousness itself. They also tell us, "You are the one you have been seeking. Stop looking elsewhere."

The final transformation occurs when we see the world without thought. Then we discover that it is never what we think, but infinitely more amazing. It is this cleansing of perception that restores the actual experience of the omnipresent divine world.

Your Story

Reflecting on your own story...

How has your life been swallowed by time and age? Has it created an experience of hopelessness and despair? How wonderful it would be to wake up from this despairing dream. When you stop thinking and dwell in pure awareness, what do you begin to notice?

What kind of yogin has come to you in times of despair? It might be an inspiration, a comment from a friend, an inner voice, or event that opens your eyes to the real possibilities of spiritual aging. It might have already happened. Can you find or imagine it?

Rahula lived sixteen more years in the awakened state of Heaven on Earth. What a boon! If this really were Heaven on Earth, how might you experience your life?

Meeting the Goddess

Opening to Love

We encountered the divine feminine in many guises and circumstances in previous stories. Now she takes center stage. In this tale from Hawaii, we meet an old man whose sole purpose in his final years is to come face-to-face with a most ferocious femme fatal. Leaving home and hearth, with no guarantees, he sets out to meet the Goddess.

She watched the old man paddle slowly to shore. When he stepped unsteadily from his dugout canoe, the man's unkempt appearance was shocking – long gray hair, thin arms and legs, deep tan, bleached shorts and worn out Hawaiian shirt. A stick figure scarecrow in baggy clothes, he looked 100 years old.

"What are you doing?" the girl asked the old man. "Where are you from?"

After catching his breath and pulling his canoe onto the sand, the old man replied, "My name is Kalapana. Kauai is my home. I forgot how long it takes to reach Hawai'i. But the winds were at my back and the sea was calm. And here I am. What is this place called?"

"You have come to Puna. But you are alone. Why have you come here? Are you visiting relatives?"

"I have come to see Pele atop Kilauea Volcano. All my life I have wanted to meet the goddess of the volcano. I promised long ago that I would not cut my hair until I met her. That was my commitment to her. So much has happened in the meantime but now I am here.

"Kalapana, it is getting late. And you look like you could use some rest and some nourishment. Come home with me. My parents are simple farmers but we have room for you and can share our catch and harvest. Come."

Gratefully, the old man followed the girl over the sand and past the palm trees up a little trail to her home. The girl's parents greeted Kalapana warmly. After sharing their evening meal, the old man slept for twelve hours.

The old man awoke with a start. It was time to find Pele. As he prepared his simple belongings, the little girl asked, "What are you doing, Kalapana? Have you looked up at the mountain? It is covered with fog and clouds. You will lose your way or fall. Wait another day. Wait until the sun shines on the mountain top."

Kalapana knew the girl was right and waited by the sea, as if counting each wave until he was free. In the afternoon, he began exploring the island, smiling at the children and greeting the families as they worked. Some asked about his long gray hair, and he patiently explained his promise to Pele. People smiled cheerfully and seemed to enjoy the old man. Some boys, however, made jokes to each other about this funny-looking man and whispered mischievously.

The day passed, and another night, but the next morning, the volcano remained enshrouded in clouds and the old man waited again. Finally, on the third day, the little girl awakened him. "Kalapana, the sky is clear. Sun shines on the mountain. It is a good day to meet Pele." She gave him a basket of food and watched as he hurried up the mountain trail into the distance.

Part way up the trail, Kalapana stopped for lunch and marveled at the beauty of the island below. After resting briefly, he resumed his trek, climbing cheerfully past lava flows, high desert, and through canyons. Up and up he went, following the winding trail, as the day grew hotter. A welcoming cloud peered over the mountain top, bringing its refreshing shade, but soon the air grew cool and the cloud showed its dark underbelly. The rains came quickly, turning into a thunderous downpour, nearly blinding him. As the sky continued to darken, Kalapana had no choice but to return.

Wet and exhausted, the old man found his way back to the village and explained his defeat to the girl's family. Kind and understanding, they encouraged Kalapana to rest and wait for another day. The next day was clear and the man started out again. His legs were strong and *his heart filled with joy. Today would be the day he met Pele. But again, out of nowhere, the rains came and Kalapana was forced to turn around. When he reached the village, the little girl said, "Maybe Pele doesn't want you to see her. Maybe she sends the storms to keep you away." The old man was too tired and discouraged to talk with the girl. Instead, he went to bed and fell into a deep and dreamless asleep.*

Early the next morning, with the very first rays of sun, Kalapana heard someone calling his name. At first, he thought the sun had burst through the small window. Then he saw a woman standing before him, more beautiful than any woman he had ever seen. Her skirt was red like fire but her face shone with light and kindness. And he knew who had come for him.

Pele said, "Here I am, Kalapana. I came to see you. It was me who sent the storms. I did not want you to fall into the fire of the volcano. But Kalapana, why did you cut your hair? You made a promise." Kalapana was shocked. "My hair?" And she was right. While he was asleep, someone had cut his hair. He smelled something burned. Then he understood - they had used fire to cut off his long gray strands. Pele continued, "Kalapana, do not worry. I know you did not break your promise. The boys in the village did this. So your punishment will only be that you must remain here in Puna for the rest of your days." After what seemed like a moment in eternity, Pele's image faded like smoke.

Kalapana sat still for several minutes. He did not care about his hair. He had seen Pele. She had revealed her beauty and her love. His lifelong dream had been fulfilled. Eventually, he found the little girl and her parents and shared his experience. They were filled with gladness and asked him to live permanently with them. "You can help with our daughter in the garden while we fish."

And so Kalapana lived in Puna for the rest of his days. He seemed to glow with happiness and everyone came to know his story. "My dream is fulfilled," he thought to himself. "Pele showed me her face. I am happy." The old man became part of the village, playing with the children and helping in gardens. Even the mischievous boys grew to love the old man. He became a legend in the village, and so they called their home Kalapana.

Interpretation

Pele, the shape-shifting and incendiary volcano goddess, is said to live in the fire pit of Kilauea volcano on the big island of Hawaii. Her name means molten lava, which she sends in rivers down to the sea. Passionate and hot-tempered, she was exiled as a child by own father for her violent outbursts. She now expresses her wrath and jealousy through fiery eruptions and most of her lovers do not survive their time with her. It is strange, then, that this old man would spend his final years dreaming of meeting her. Perhaps he knew something others do not.

Can you imagine paddling over 80 miles alone in open seas from Kauai to Hawai'i just to meet a volcano goddess? The answer depends on your motives. Kalapana does not wish a romantic liaison with Pele, an exceedingly risky endeavor for anyone, and his romantic passions have long since retired. He is determined to see her for another reason, so determined that he makes a commitment not to cut his hair until he does. If he were a young man, hair might symbolize sexual energy or virility; as an old man, however, his long, unkempt gray locks may instead symbolize spiritual development, the wisdom of a long life, and perhaps the expression of his feminine side. In sum, with respect and wisdom, Kalapana seeks an audience with the divine feminine to complete his life. He knows the risk he is taking. He is probably even willing to die for this moment. This is the way to approach a powerful goddess.

Pele blocks Kalapana's journey several times, first to protect him from the fire pit, which indeed burns too hot for mortal men, and second, because this meeting must be on her terms – she is a goddess, after all. But like Yama, she recognizes Kalapana's sincerity and appreciates his deep respect for her (unlike her suitors), and finally appears before him, generously opening her heart and letting her divine love pour out upon him. While she speaks of punishment for an act Kalapana did not commit, the punishment is only to stay in his new home with his new family; less a punishment than a symbol of the changed consciousness he achieved after completing his quest.

Why did Kalapana seek an audience with Pele? As we have seen, one of the great tasks of aging is to balance masculine and feminine energies in a new and mature unity, a marriage of opposites that dissolves duality. Kalapana intuitively understands this imperative and, like the Hindu tradition of leaving home and family to seek the divine in old age, he has paddled for days to experience the blessing of the divine feminine. As he takes this experience inside himself, he is changed. He embodies her love and blesses all he meets. Kalapana's very presence now creates Heaven on Earth for others. He is full of love. He is home. He has the goddess inside him.

Conclusions

This short and poignant story is about the quest for love – specifically, the quest to complete our life with the love of divinity shining through us. Merging masculine and feminine, consciousness and being, secular and sacred, we embody divinity and awaken the energies of love. This is what Kalapana knew intuitively in his aging experience. It was his last quest. In meeting the goddess, he opened himself completely to her love, which then flowed through him to others. This is how Elders change the world and create Heaven on Earth. Kalapana did this with such simple sincerity that all who came into his presence felt blessed and loved.

Reflections

During her four-year decline, I spoke with my mother every week and visited her monthly from two states away. In spite of her dementia-related language difficulties, she began to express a simple, kind, and almost transpersonal love. In this new and radiant consciousness, I believe I met the divine feminine, and her presence shines inside me. As a result, I am changing, embodying a kind of love that transcends conditions, identities, and beliefs. In sum, my mother released the crusading extravert I knew as a child, the fierce goddess of social activism, and became instead a gentle goddess of light and love. Perhaps this was the purpose of her dementia, to steadily dissolve the ego's power for the purpose of revealing something very different – the transparency of divine love.

Your Story

Reflecting on your own story…

What do you long for to complete your life? How does it involve love

How might time and erosion wear down your ego in the journey of aging to allow the goddess of love to become a divine light within you? How will you love unconditionally?

Imagine you have completed your personality and felt the pure love of the divine Self now residing inside you. How would you be different in the world? How would the world seem different to you?

Periwinkle and the Old Man

Choosing Our Fate

From my grandmother comes this simple yet beautiful story written for me more than a half century ago. Her tale is about the profound challenge of following the heart during the long journey of life, and the pain of losing our way, as Owain did, and as we all do on the long and winding road of life. It tells us again about the search for divine love that is so important to the spirituality of aging – as Kanapala demonstrated – and how its consciousness changes our experience of the journey and the world.

As I sat on the patio one morning, watching my grandsons at play, one of them climbed an orange tree and shook the branches, hoping that some ripe oranges would fall to the ground. A few oranges fell down. Then, to my surprise, something green flew out of the tree. Dear me, I thought, has someone lost a little parrot, and has the parrot flown into our orange trees? Then the green thing started flying toward me, and I saw, to my astonishment, that it was not a bird. But what was it? Why, it was Periwinkle, my little fairy friend.

"Periwinkle," I cried. "What are you doing here? And you look so troubled. What ever is the matter?"

Periwinkle spoke immediately, his words tumbling out in pain. "Someone told me that people no longer believe in fairies," he said. "If everyone stops believing in fairies, there will be no fairies. Fairies cannot live unless people think of them and believe in them. In this age of science and reason, of 'facing the facts,' I heard that very few people even think of fairies. Because fairies cannot be made, or proved, by laboratory experiment, people say they do not exist."

"But Periwinkle that is absurd," I said. "Lots of things exist that we cannot see; like the air we breathe and the music we hear and the

thoughts we think. Some of the most real, the most important, the most wonderful, things in life are the things we cannot see; like friendship and love and kindness. And there will always be children who believe in fairies. Children will always believe.

"I am glad to hear you say that," said Periwinkle in relief. "But may I tell you a story that my mother tells, about a little boy who made the fairies miserable because he stopped believing in them?"

I nodded my consent.

"This boy," began Periwinkle, "did not believe in fairies. At least not after someone told him that fairies did not exist. Before that, he had loved fairies, and the fairies had loved him. They had played with him, and told him stories; and he had played with them, and told them stories. But after he stopped believing in fairies, he could not tell good stories any more. He could no longer think about the make believe of fairies and giants and witches. Gradually he forgot how to make believe. He forgot how to imagine stories in his mind.

The boy grew up. He met a beautiful girl. He loved her and she loved him. He wanted to ask her to marry him but he was afraid her love for him was too good to be true. He was afraid that he just imagined that she was kind and beautiful. He must be making it up in his mind. No one, he thought, should imagine anything. So he went away, and left the beautiful girl and all the happiness they could have had together.

She was very sad when he left her, because she loved him too. She finished her college work, and became a teacher in a school. She taught there many years, and finally became principal of the school. Some years later she died.

The man lived alone. He worked hard for forty years; and became a big man in the world. He was wealthy and important and admired. Many people said, 'Look at this man, what a success in material things.' He had everything that money could buy; but he was a very lonely man. He was an unhappy man. He had nothing but the things he could touch or prove or see.

After long years of material success his health began to give way.

He became a sick man. For some weeks he stayed in a hospital. When he was better, his doctor told him to go where it was warm, so he went to Florida. He tried to rest, but he was restless. There was nothing for him to do. He had forgotten how to play or think about the things that bring happiness, like love and friendship and giving pleasure to others.

One day, as he was sitting in the garden of his hotel, he saw a little boy playing. The little boy ran here and there, and kept talking. The old man watched the little boy for a while and wondered whom he was talking to. So, when the boy came near him, he beckoned to him and said, 'Who are you talking to little boy?'

The boy answered, 'To my friend, to Nimble-Trimble.'

The old man asked, 'Who is Nimble-Trimble, and where is he? I do not see anyone, anywhere.'

The little boy answered, 'Right there,' pointing in front of him. 'There is Nimble-Trimble. There is my fairy friend Nimble-Trimble. Can't you see him?'

The old man drew himself up stiffly and said, 'No I cannot see him. Nobody sees fairies. There are no fairies. You are just a silly little boy.'

The smile vanished from the little boy's face; and his eyes filled with tears.

'No fairies!' he said, 'No Nimble-Trimble!'

He stood bewildered for a moment. Then, indignantly, he said, 'Of course there are fairies! He added, 'Of course there is Nimble-Trimble but...' and his voice changed to dismay. 'Look, Nimble-Trimble has fallen down: you have hurt him.'

The little boy pointed to the ground. There lay the fairy Nimble-Trimble. He lay very still; almost as though he were dead; as though the man's hard words had killed him.

The little boy bent over him.

'Nimble-Trimble,' he said, 'get up! Are you hurt? Are you sick? What has happened to you?'

Nimble-Trimble said very faintly, 'The man's words knocked me down. The man's thoughts are going to kill me.'

The little boy said, 'No Nimble-Trimble, the man's thoughts cannot kill you when I am here. I know you are a fairy. I know that you are my friend. I know that you live. I need you Nimble-Trimble. You must not die. You must live with me.'

The little boy bent over the fairy, and took him by the hand. He helped him to his feet. Nimble-Trimble rose slowly and smiled at the little boy.

The old man turned his head away from the little boy, when the boy had spoken of fairies; but he could not help hearing what the boy had been saying to the fairy. Suddenly an old forgotten memory came back to him of fairies he had seen and played with long ago. Like a ray of sunshine they came to his mind. He could see them now. Slowly the tense tired expression on the man's face changed. He almost smiled.

He turned toward the boy; and he saw that the boy was lifting something from the ground. What was it? Why it was a fairy! A real fairy, and he had not seen one in over sixty years.

The man turned his head away again quickly. Of course it was not a fairy. Of course it could not be true. He was just imagining it. Perhaps he was sicker than he thought. He had better see his doctor.

A dimness came over the old man's eyes. He couldn't see anything. His head fell to one side.

The little boy looked at him. Perhaps he is asleep, he thought, that cross old man. He walked away. The fairy flew after him.

When the old man regained consciousness the boy and the fairy had gone. My heart, he thought to himself. My heart is playing tricks on me again. What is the use of trying to get well, when a little thing like that boy and his fairy upset me? He thought he would like to get up and go back to the hotel, but he was not strong enough to rise. I will wait a few minutes until my strength comes back, he said.

He felt a gentle touch on his shoulder. He looked up. An angel was standing beside him. The angel was very beautiful. The angel's face was exceptionally beautiful. Where had he seen that face before? What was his mind doing to him that morning! Why couldn't he remember the face? Then it all came back to him. The beautiful girl he had loved years ago. Yes, she had that face: but what was the face doing here beside him? Why was the face on an angel? What was the matter with him, seeing angels and fairies in one morning? Was he going crazy? He must see his doctor again.

In his anxiety he tried once more to rise. He could not. His legs were too weak to hold him. His head was spinning.

The angel spoke very gently.

'You will be all right,' she said, 'you will be all right now. If only you could have believed long ago, you would have been so much happier; and you would have made other people happy. See how happy that little boy was in believing.'

'I was told not to believe long ago,' said the man stiffly.

'I know,' answered the angel. 'That was your misfortune.'

'But I could not have gone on believing in fairies for ever,' said the man. 'All children stop believing in fairies some time.'

'Yes they do,' said the angel, 'but they can still believe in the thoughts and happiness of little children; and fairies are in the thoughts and happiness of little children.'

'I suppose they are,' said the old man faintly, 'my happiness in fairies was taken away from me when I was very young.'

'It was too bad,' said the angel, 'because it prevented you from the gradual change of thought: the gradual change from thinking about fairies that are alive to fairies that are in the mind. It kept you from believing in many other wonderful things such as,' (the angel spoke more slowly), 'such as your love for the girl and her love for you.'

'Perhaps that is true,' said the old man. 'I loved a beautiful girl once'

'I know,' whispered the angel.

'I thought loving her was too good to be true,' said the man. 'I could not believe that such happiness could be mine.'

'Yes,' said the angel, 'so you ran away from your happiness, and deprived her of hers.'

'It is too late now,' said the man, 'I am old.'

'It is never too late to love, and believe, and to trust in your belief,' said the angel.

The old man sat silent for a moment. He looked at the angel.

'You are beautiful,' he said, 'as beautiful as she was.'

He looked at the angel for a long time.

Finally he seemed to understand something he had not understood before. Suddenly the sun seemed to shine upon him.

'Are you the beautiful girl I lost long ago?'

'I am,' said the angel.

'I am old,' said the man, 'nobody will want me now. I am an old man.'

'You are only as old as you allow yourself to be,' said the angel.

'I am too old to live any more,' said the man.

'To live as you are, yes,' said the angel: 'too old to live as you are, but not too old to live as you're going to be. If you will believe and if you will trust in your belief, you can be young again.'

'My body can never be young again,' said the man.

'No, not your body,' said the angel, 'but your mind. Your mind and spirit can be young again. You body does not matter now.'

They were silent for a few moments, the old man and the angel.

'It is a long time since I have seen you,' he said.

'Yes it is a long time,' answered the angel. 'I have waited a long time.'

'A long time,' repeated the old man, in a whisper.

'God has waited a long time,' said the angel. 'God has waited for you a long time. He has waited for you to see the beautiful world that he has given you to live in, and for you to believe in the beauty and goodness of His gifts.'

'I must have been a fool,' said the old man, 'to keep Him waiting so long.

'You were,' said the angel, 'we all are, at times.'

'It is too late. I have waited too long,' said the man.

'It is never too late,' said the angel. 'It is never too long.'

'Will God take me as I am,' asked the man. 'I have so little to give Him. I have given everything to the world I have lived in.'

'He will take you as you are,' replied the angel.

She held out her hand.

'Will you lead me to Him,' said the man.

'That is what I came for,' said the angel.

He gave her his hand. He rose to his feet.

'Oh, it is easier now,' he said. 'It is easier to walk now.'

'That is because you are walking in the right direction,' said the
angel.

She led him away.

"Pool old man," I said. "Think of what he missed."

"Yes," said Periwinkle. "Think of what he missed all his life."

Interpretation

The problem addressed in this story – whether fairies would still exist if people stopped believing – is important at two levels. At a personal level, my parents were products of "science and reason," gladly embracing the "cold hard facts" of scientific materialism after centuries of religious dogma. In the modern age of reason, knowledge was defined by ideas that could be proven, replicated and empirically applied – my parents did not believe in fairies or God. My grandmother was gently cautioning me to keep an open mind about the unseen world of imagination. She was helping a little boy build a bridge from the magical world of childhood to the realism of adults, without surrendering his dreams and the imagination that carries his life forward.

What are fairies after all? The word "fairy" derives from the Latin word "fata" meaning fate, suggesting the existence of an unseen spirit world behind the workings of destiny. "Fairies" are creations from the collective unconscious, that transpersonal realm of universal images, themes, and archetypes that give meaning to existence. Their magical function in the psyche is not only to enchant and instruct us, but also to guide us back to the divine world we surrender when thought and belief replace the direct perception of Eden. If we refuse this journey home, we remain, like the old man, ossified in cynicism.

My grandmother was also wise enough to understand that the problem of disbelief cannot be solved by fairies; the answer comes from the realization that the inner world that creates fairies is innate to human nature and can never be destroyed. But it can be betrayed. As we see with the old man, there is a terrible cost in betraying the journey of the heart hidden revealed in our imagination. Had the little boy in the Elder-Tree Mother rejected the old man's story, he might never have understood the value of remembrance. Sadly, this betrayal is also part of the universal story, for we each miss years of life's magic believing that only what we have or accomplish really counts.

Conclusions

Children bring us back to the enchanted world late in life, after we have given up the urgency of the middle years, because they still live there. Playing with young children, we see again "the beautiful world" fashioned by divinity – the Heaven on Earth anticipated in our hearts. This story suggests that the man began moving into the divine world when he saw the little boy's fairy, and again when his anima, symbolized as the angel (and representing his own divine essence) arrived. What if the old man had stayed a little longer in this awakened consciousness before dying? Would he have discovered Heaven on Earth before departing? Leaving this world for Heaven in the next world is the old story; the new one tells us that Heaven on Earth might also be found right here by lifting the veil of thought.

How do we reconcile the goal of dissolving thought and fantasy in pure consciousness – the advice of Yama, Krishna and Rahulu's yogin, with the urging of the Elder-Tree Mother and my own grandmother that we never give up the inner world of imagination and symbols? Isn't my grandmother advising us to remain in the deluded state of maya? Here is my answer: fairy tales and myths symbolically encode a secret map of life's long journey, a map we receive at birth. As we have seen throughout these preceding stories, this map symbolically "explains" why things happen and what they really mean. Created from the experiences of thousands of generations, this map is stored in the images and stories comprising the collective unconscious. Because we all lose the Eden of early childhood, my grand-mother's fairy tale urges us to hold onto love, beauty and the heart's desire, for they lead back to the divine world. What she did not realize, however, was that the traditional fairy tale ends too early. With our revolutionary longevity, a new stage of spiritual life has been created. As we will see in our next tale, Elders are meant to wake up from the dream of life and discover who and where we really are.

Reflections

I certainly agree with my grandmother that the intangibles of love and imagination contribute to the beauty and value of life. In loving, the divine flows into the world through us, and with our imagination, we see and create all that is possible from love. Sadly, thought and imagination can also create immense suffering, with frightening beliefs about suffering, danger, scarcity, enemies, illness, and threat leading to greed, compe-tition, and war. Dissolving this fearful, thought-driven mode of perception in pure consciousness, however, opens the flow of divine love and generosity, and literally changes our perception of the world from Hell to Heaven. Fairy tales teach us how this transformational journey works, until we begin to wake up, exit the labyrinth of mind, and see that we are already home.

My awakening has been slow but steady. My practice is simple – I remind myself to stop thinking, heighten awareness, focus on the divine Presence (pure consciousness), and merge consciousness and being. Then I watch the world turn back into Heaven on Earth right before my eyes. Joy and love flow from this embodying of divinity. Aging has provided the space to devote myself to this practice of awakening. It has been a gift of immeasurable value. I believe Elders are meant to be the carriers of this light into the world. My grandmother was such an Elder.

Your Story

Reflecting on your own story...

Did reason, science, superficial values, or some other authority convince you to deny your love and betray your dream at some time in your life? What happened and what was the result?

What were the most important fairies or angels in your life - the ultimate symbols of love, meaning, or divine purpose inside you? How did you continue to believe in them in the face of life's ups and downs?

Can you imagine meeting this kind of angel as you near death? What would she tell you about your life?

The Color Tree

A New Story of Aging

Once I recognized the paucity of fairy tales pertaining to this revolutionary new stage of aging, I began to think I should write my own. If my grandmother could write fairy tales in her sixties, why not me, as well? I see my grandmother smile as I say this. But where would a new fairy tale come from? How would I find it? The answer, of course, is obvious – it will come from the same place all fairy tales originate. But this story cannot be forced or pre-determined, for as the wise old story-teller explained, a real fairy tale comes knocking on your forehead only when it is ready.

I wanted to invite a modern day fairy tale, not one from olden times. I began to imagine a story set in the context of a common and familiar aging experience – hospitalization. I have been in the hospital seven times with atrial fibrillation in the past ten years and know it well. I also recently faced the possibility of bone marrow cancer, a bleak prospect if true. Now I was ready! Just like the sick little boy in the Little Elder-Tree Mother, I awaited a story compatible with my own experience.

As the old man grew a tree in a teapot in that tale, transforming a boy's sick room into an extraordinary preview of his life, I let the magic of spontaneous story telling transform my hospital scenario into an adventure in spiritual awakening. In a way, this story builds on my grandmother's tale but then allows the protagonist to explore the remarkable spirituality of this new stage of life. I chose a female protagonist to better balance the gender representation in the book, but more importantly, to close with a tale conceived from the feminine presence, sorely missing in the fairy tales and consciousness of our time.

The old woman lay in the hospital bed – cool oxygen flowing through a clear plastic tube into her nose, an I.V. of heart-stabilizing medication in her hand, and a beeping heart monitor near her bed. She had been in cardiac intensive care for three days following a heart attack and emergency bypass surgery. The other bed in the room was empty.

It was 2:00 am and the old woman could not stop thinking about her situation. She felt weak from the surgery. What am I going to do? Who will care for me when I am discharged? She lived alone but her three grown daughters would circle the wagons around her and insist she live with one of them – a loss of personal control she was not ready for.

Unable to sleep, she finally rang for a nurse. No one came. In a few minutes she rang again. She felt alone in the world. Nighttime in a hospital ward is a strange and surreal experience. Eerie artificial light, distant indecipherable sounds, the loneliness of your own thoughts – it was as if time and the world stood still, or abandoned her altogether. Where is that nurse?!

Was it her imagination or did someone turn up the light a little? A gentle brightness spread down the hall and into her room. That certainly wouldn't help her insomnia. And the air seemed to change, as if charged with some subtle and indescribable energy. Then her heart monitor fell silent. The mind plays tricks in the middle of the night in a place like this, she thought. Probably the medications. But the old woman also felt a strange excitement, the way she felt as a child on Christmas Eve. Then she saw him – a pleasant-looking male nurse in starched white uniform coming around the corner into her room.

"Hello Mrs. Winchester. Why you're wide awake!" he exclaimed. "You should be asleep. Can I get you anything?" He almost glowed. That was strange.

Her mind felt slow and dull next to his cheerful banter. "I can't sleep. Don't know why."

"Something bothering you? Want to talk a while? Sometimes talking helps."

The old woman immediately began to feel calmer, almost peaceful. That was strange. Something about this nurse put her in such a good mood. "Maybe you can help me," she said finally. I don't know what I'm going to do when they discharge me."

The nurse came over to her bedside, straightened her blanket, and checked her forehead for fever. Something happened when his hand touched her skin, something profoundly comforting, and he left it there for a moment longer. Now she felt she could tell him anything, and so she began.

"I had a heart attack last week and almost died. I felt the coldness of death and was so incredibly afraid. But now, with you, I don't feel so frightened. I don't know why I'm saying this but for the first time in my life, I'm wondering what death might be like. It doesn't scare me like before. Everybody dies, it's part of life, it's just natural, and maybe even easy. And now that I'm older, it seems more like a friend. In fact, it feels like I have already died somehow and the old me is gone. But it also seems like some kind of beginning, like I'm fine, maybe better than fine. Am I crazy?"

"No. I think you're just having a new experience of yourself. What else do you notice?"

"Well, it's hard to describe. It's like I'm so much more conscious. I'm aware of things around me but, strangely, even more aware of the awareness, like the things I see are not nearly as important as consciousness itself. And I no longer feel concerned with my old self, which suddenly feels now like an old, worn-out idea that is fading away. Now, without this self, there are no limits, no boundaries, nothing separating me from everything. It's like I took off a overly-tight jacket. And I feel this huge love. Why is this happening? I feel like I am turning inside out."

"It sounds like you are discovering your original nature, Mrs. Winchester. This is who you really are when you're not caught up in your confining self and its limiting worried thoughts."

"My heart attack, it wasn't such a bad thing after all. It's like it broke open a cocoon and now my awareness is expanding into this

amazing new experience of freedom and love."

"It is your heart opening, Mrs. Winchester. Like most people, you thought of yourself as a separate little consciousness in a lonely universe. You are breaking out of this mental prison. It happens when we release our old familiar identity and discover the full and real nature of consciousness. That's why you had the heart attack – to let go of your old self and wake up."

"And the world itself suddenly seems different now," the old woman continued, "more beautiful, more radiant, more amazing. Everything around me shimmers with radiance. Even this hospital is full of light now, like a heavenly palace. Everything blazes with the light of eternity. What's wrong with me? I'm talking like a crazy mystic!"

"Yes you are! This is what they see. When you wake up from the shadowy illusions of human life, you discover that God – called by whatever name you like – is everywhere, everything, every place. And that direct experience of divinity completely changes how your see the world, for now everything is alive, conscious and holy. These realizations simply reflect your awakening."

The nurse bent down and kissed her forehead. "I have to go now. You'll be fine. Just relax and enjoy this evolving experience." The old woman lay speechless as she watched him walk away to resume his other "duties." The old woman was not sure whether sleep ever came that night, so excited was she with this new awareness.

Mrs. Winchester was discharged the next day. She convinced her daughters that it was safe to return to her apartment by the park. But the world was different now. Everything seemed pregnant with divinity. Rapt with fascination, she would stroll through the park exploring the ever-changing life of plants, insects, and critters, and seemed to make friends with all of them. She felt like St. Francis communing with the birds, squirrels and bees. Sunsets became sacred paintings, nature sounds were heavenly symphonies, and life was an ongoing experience in a divine world. She had stumbled into Heaven on Earth. It was unbelievable.

Then she noticed it – this immense tree. Not like any other tree she had ever seen. This tree was majestic – its boughs full and widely branching, dressed in the most amazing leaves, like the fall colors you find in the northeastern United States, except even more glorious. Iridescent hues of red, gold, yellow, orange, purple, and brown shimmered in the breezes, periodically producing cascading sparks of colored light accompanied by barely audible tinkling sounds and the most heavenly fragrances imaginable. A choir of birdsong filled the air. This tree, she thought, grows in the middle of the park as the Tree of Life grew in the Garden of Eden. This realization took her breath away.

Then the old woman had another thought: I must share this vision of beauty with others. Getting up from the park bench, she looked around and spotted a young woman sitting on another bench fussing over two adorable little boys.

"Hello," she cried out as she approached, "Have you seen the tree in the park? The one with all the colors and smells? Isn't it astounding! And your children. They are so beautiful. They look like angels from Heaven!" Despite her excitement, the old woman tried to act normal. After all, she did not wish to upset this mother or her children.

The young woman looked up at her with a mixture of fear, bewilderment and surprise. Was this lady crazy, intoxicated, or just senile? Can't she see that I have my hands full with these restless kids? The children just received their vaccinations at the pediatrician's office and I have a full day of grocery shopping, meal planning, and a late afternoon appointment at the beauty parlor. Plus my husband recently mentioned something about possibly his losing his job at the bank. What would we do then? Oh God I do not have time for some crazy old bag lady from the park.

"What do you want?" the young woman asked. Are you selling something? Is this about a handout? I'm sorry. I don't have time. I have to go."

The old woman was puzzled by this abrupt rebuff, but then, as if from some newly-acquired ESP, she understood: the young woman was preoccupied, tired, and overwhelmed. An image arose of her tossing and turning all night after a fight with her husband over money. With a thousand worried thoughts on her mind, she was not going to see the beauty of the park or the tree today. She called out an apology to the rapidly departing woman, turned, and walked toward the city.

Across the street began the city's financial district. People moved briskly in the bright sunshine, energized by a sense of purpose and importance. Stepping onto the sidewalk, the old woman collided with a well-dressed businessman rushing somewhere. The man's briefcase dropped from his hand and broke open on the sidewalk, spilling its contents everywhere. Growling a string of expletives, he bent down to pick up his papers.

"I'm so sorry," said the old woman. Here, let me help you."

"Leave me alone, you old crone. You've done enough already." With a nearly maniacal gleam in his eyes, the businessman repacked his briefcase and hurried off. He was unstoppable.

Again, as if from some new clairvoyance, the old woman understood: All the businessman wanted was money. With countless plans for acquiring wealth, he viewed the people in his life as objects to be used, manipulated and discarded, like machine parts, on the way to his fortune. And she "saw" something else: the businessman as a child, cowering before an enraged father ridiculing a painting he had brought home from school. Art was a waste of time to his father. All that counted was financial success. The old woman felt the sadness hidden beneath the businessman's crazed ambitions. Though beauty lay all around him, he could not see it.

Oh well, thought the old woman. I need to find a place where love and spiritual wisdom open people's eyes to the world's wondrous beauty and perfection. She looked around and saw a church several blocks away. Of course, she thought. That's where I will find kindred souls!

Passing an alley, someone whispered, "Please, mam, can you help me." The old woman looked into the darkness and saw a man with a child. After a moment's hesitation, she walked toward them. Passing a dumpster full of garbage, she was suddenly yanked into shadowy darkness and felt a knife press against his neck. "Give me your purse, your watch, and anything else of value – NOW." The old woman did what she was told. The cry for help had been a trick. But with her new psychic sense, the old woman saw "into" her attacker's life: this man was hateful, cynical, and impulsive. Believing that he had been cheated by a miserable childhood, he could justify any kind of brutality, selfishness or criminal act. The boy with him was just a tool for his scam. Drugs, alcohol and a "good time" would be the rewards of his cruelty. But this man's energy was more than just hurt and anger, it felt evil and the old woman was glad to be free from its hold.

As her attacker blended nonchalantly back into the crowds, the old woman pondered the morning's experiences. The world human beings create can often be filled with suffering and misunderstanding, she thought. Depression, worry, greed, bitterness, and hatred had consumed the consciousness of those she had met in the past five minutes. This was not Heaven on Earth for them, this was Hell on Earth. As if needing renewed hope, the old woman looked back toward the park and that wonderful tree. Something had changed. The tree's radiance had dimmed noticeably.

Undaunted, however, the old woman finally reached the church. She stepped into its cool, dark interior and waited for her eyes to adjust. Near the front, she noticed the minister talking quietly with an older gentleman who walked away. The old woman approached the minister and asked, "Do you have a minute? I have something really important to tell you."

"Of course. What's on your mind?" asked the minister.

Words gushed out of the old woman like a torrent. "I have seen the Garden. I have witnessed what looks like the Tree of Life in the Garden of Eden and I see divinity everywhere. I almost died from a heart attack but now I have found a new life flooded with light and love. Can you help me understand what has happened to me?"

The minister looked closely at the old woman. Who is this lady? She's too well dressed to be a street person but she's talking crazy, babbling on and on about the Garden of Eden. There's no Garden of Eden out there. Maybe I can talk her into attending our service or bible class.

"No really, I see God everywhere," the old woman exclaimed. "Don't you see the beauty, the radiance? And that tree in the park! Come look. It's on fire."

Now I know she's nuts, thought the minister. There's no fire in the park and I just don't have time for another wacky drop-in. "Mam," the minister said, "come back later for our introductory bible lessons. Perhaps they will help you understand." The minister's demeanor then changed a little, his eyes grew shrewd and zealous, his mind whirred with grandiose possibilities. "Wait a minute," he said. "I believe you may be possessed and I will cure you with the power of the holy spirit. I can exorcize the devil and bring you to Jesus. Are you willing?"

"What devil?" the old woman asked. There's no devil. There is just beauty and light and joy. What are you talking about?" Looking into the minister's eyes, the old woman shivered. Something was very wrong here. This minister looked possessed himself. She did not want see any further into this man's life; instead the old woman turned and ran out of the church into the sunshine. Its warmth gradually calmed her fear. Things were getting too crazy!

Nearby was a pleasant looking young man. Thank goodness, the old woman said to herself, someone sane and normal. The young man was gazing at a display of exotic destinations in a travel agency window.

"Thinking about taking a trip?" asked the old woman.

The young man did not answer but seemed to pull away slightly. "Are you ok?"

Again no response and the youth begin moving away. Right then a vision opened in the old woman's consciousness: a picture of a distant, sad and lonely person who felt invisible and awkward, who retreated into a posture of social conformity to avoid conflict. He was a follower with no opinions of his own. He, too, had no idea of the beauty and love that surrounded him. Instead, his eyes were dull and dead. He knew nothing but self-loathing. Slowly he moved down the street.

Things were not going well for the old woman. Once more she turned toward the park to draw inspiration from the glowing tree, but its colors had dulled even further. Had the tree's beauty been a medication side effect? Then one more idea came to the old woman. The university! A place of knowledge, intelligence and curiosity. Surely someone there would be interested in her glorious tree!

A short bus trip brought her to the university grounds. Grand arches, ivy-covered Victorian architecture, eager students and brilliant professors. By chance, she walked by a small seminar of graduate students meeting outside. They were discussing the philosophy of science. How inspiring, she thought, and listened in. The professor was eloquent and informed, the students perceptive, but the lecture shocked her. Skepticism, intellectual superiority, scientific materialism - these were the cornerstones of his presentation. "We can only know what can be measured," the professor was saying. "All other questions are useless and fall in the realm of religion or super-stition." It was a barren philosophy that discounted the power of mystery, beauty and wonder. The students were literally sitting in the Garden of Eden dismissing the value of rapture. The old woman turned and walked slowly back across town to the park.

It was late afternoon now; the world was growing dark and gloomy. Rush hour was picking up. The sounds of cars, construction, and cell phone conversations echoed down the cold canyons of steel and glass. The old woman was particularly irritated by the screaming sounds of power tools ahead. God, she thought, is there no peace on Earth here? Then she saw it: men with chain saws tearing into the magnificent tree. She rushed toward them.

"What are you doing?" the old woman yelled. "Leave that tree alone. Can't you see its beauty?"

"Back off lady," a rough and sweaty man warned. "The tree has got to go. A new office building's going in here. You can't stand in the way of progress!"

"No, no, no," the old woman shouted. "Please no." She let out an anguished cry that seemed to rock the universe. "No, no, no…!" Then all went black until she heard a voice somewhere in the distance.

"Mrs. Winchester, Mrs. Winchester, wake up. You're been having a bad dream. Everything is ok. You're safe in the hospital. Please calm down."

The old woman looked around. There she was, sitting up in her hospital bed in the same room. She had never left. Confused and disoriented, she fell back on her pillow and gave up.

Mrs. Winchester was discharged for real the next day. As none of her daughters could get off work to pick her up, she was on her own. Suitcase in hand, alone and despondent, she trudged out the front door. The world hadn't changed. It was the same dreary city that had broken her heart. With no better place to go, the old woman walked slowly, head down, toward the park, hoping to find a quiet bench to collect her thoughts. The grass was wet and the path winding. But suddenly, looking up, there it was. THE TREE. The same tree she had seen in her dream. Bursting with colors, fragrance and birdsong. Huge and magnificent. Her heart broke open. It was still there, still real.

The old woman rushed to the base of the tree, where an aura of grace and energy held her in a timeless love. She fell to her knees and cried and cried and cried. Happy, relieved, and amazed, yet still afraid it might only be another dream. Comforted by the tree's presence, the old woman finally relaxed. Her shoulders dropped, her mind grew quiet. All she wanted now was to sit in the gentle embrace of this tree.

A tap on her right shoulder surprised the old woman. She turned to see a little boy perhaps six or seven years old. "Hi," said the boy, who smiled and reached out to touch the tree. "I love this tree," he said. "She is my friend and she loves me back. She shows me how beautiful life is." Then, to old woman's even greater surprise, the

97

little boy cried out, "Grampa, Grampa, come see our tree. Isn't she beautiful today." An elderly man, with white hair and a cane, ambled over to the boy. "Oh she is in her most colorful dress today, and so full of love," he said. "And who is your new friend?"

Time stopped. The world around her began to brighten, perception sharpened, beauty was again everywhere. The park lit up in a million radiant colors. Joy exploded in her soul. Could it be? Had the old woman finally returned to the world revealed by her night nurse? She was speechless. The elderly man seemed to understand and said, "We come here everyday. Perhaps we will see you again tomorrow."

Then she heard the night nurse whisper, "You are still working things out. You are learning how to experience the divine world. It comes and goes in this phase. You lost it when your consciousness was again clouded with negative and discouraging thoughts, but now you have found Heaven on Earth again. As you tune into the divine nature of reality, mystical experiences will continue to alter your consciousness. One day you will become a teacher like me." The nurse's voice melted into the summer breeze.

The old woman sat in silence at the base of the tree for what seemed an eternity. Filled with joy, she could feel herself radiating love. It was boundless. She was love. She was an angel. She was every teacher that ever reached enlightenment and chose to stay a bit longer out of sheer love. She filled the world with her own divine presence now. She was a gift to be given everywhere. She was what old people are supposed to be.

Interpretation

A fairy tale set in a the modern world, The Color Tree infuses everyday reality with mythical and mystical possibilities, allowing the rules of physics to become elastic and fate to change a humdrum life into a divine encounter and a new world.

An old woman, representing each of us in the journey of aging, meets the divine in the guise of an enlightened night nurse and his touch initiates a revelation of the divine world.

Happening in the surreal hours of deep night, this encounter with this higher self opens her eyes to another, truer, way of seeing the world. The old woman is thrilled beyond measure but eventually falls into sleep. In the dream that follows, she must confront the many ways she – and each of us – allows worry, greed, anger, righteousness, fear, and belief to obscure the divine world we were born into. Each person she greets is a part of herself – exaggerated caricatures symbolizing the ways we habitually avoid consciousness. The old woman tries to show these various personas the beauty of divinity, but they are too self-involved to notice or care. So it is that we each hold onto grudges, wounds, defenses, or schemes no matter the cost to ourselves or those around us, until life breaks open the shell of personality and, as the saying goes, we see the light.

Can this fairy tale help us experience aging in a new way, and what might that awareness allow us to do? When we allow our mythic imagination to see events in symbolic and allegorical ways, the everyday world becomes a fairy tale with hidden – and profound – teachings. From this vantage point, we can ask, for example, whether the old woman's vision was "just" a tree in fall colors or a mythically-created opportunity to see the world in a transcendent way, one that opens the perception of Heaven on Earth. The perceptual shift associated with myth and mysticism, in other words, draws us into an awakened consciousness that transforms everything we see. The story seems to be telling us: stop thinking, wake up, and experience the world as it truly is - a divine place. This same shift is especially available to Elders who, in their retirement, suspend thinking and doing long enough to witness the astounding beauty of life everywhere. But just like the old woman, Elders also fall back into old habits of mind and emotion and lose the sight of Heaven on Earth. We each need to be reminded to wake up.

In sum, fairy tales show us the way back to our divine home. The old woman in this story finds herself in a medical crisis, but when her eyes are opened, she discovers that her divine home is everywhere and it has been there all the time. From a busy hospital in a chaotic city to the mystical awareness of Heaven on Earth, the journey is but a blink away. In aging, as the schemes, goals, and identities disappear, we have a chance to wake up, cleanse our consciousness of a lifetime of thought and belief, and see where we really are. The mystics haves been telling us for millennia that Heaven is already here when we are awake enough to see it. One of the purposes of aging is to do just that.

Reflections

This tale reminds me of a Near-Death account I read years ago. In a state of clinical death following a heart attack, this man's consciousness had left his body and moved into the afterlife. A spirit guide led him through the realms that exist after death, explaining that people are drawn to places that correspond with their emotional energy, personality and beliefs. In one dark and hellish realm, he witnessed people screaming at each other, fighting incessantly. They could not stop. What these people failed to notice were angels just above them trying to get their attention in order to lead them out of this realm. Trapped in their anger and hatred, they never looked up. At one time or another, we have all been stuck in just such self-defeating dramas.

We find Heaven on Earth when we release self-created distress and open our senses to the myth, mystery, and miracle of life. The Color Tree symbolizes this shift in perception that reveals Heaven on Earth. Like the old woman, we have glimpsed it countless times but turned away and forgotten. Before time runs out, look for the vision that will change your world.

Your Story

Reflecting on your own story...

Imagine your life or current situation as a fairy tale. What does your allegorical consciousness reveal about it?

When has an unexpected life event, like the old woman's heart attack, temporarily arrested your normal thought processes, offering an opportunity to see the world in a fresh or startling new way? What happened?

Can you recall seeing the Color Tree in one form in or another in the past and turned away? If you saw it again today, outside your window or down the street, how would you hope to respond?

Conclusions

The Three Secrets of Aging

Fairy tales are a source of deep and genuine truth. Not the scientific truth of repeated experiments, but the timeless archetypal truth of the collective unconscious, a vast treasure trove of wisdom. Once we grasp its symbolic language and tap into our own capacity for deep knowing, fairy tale and myth give us ways to access this wisdom, and we soon discover that we already understand so much more than we realize.

From England, Ireland, Denmark, India, Mesopotamia, Hawaii and America, from times past to this very moment, from my grandmother's vision and my own soul, have come ten Bedtime Stories for Elders. What do they mean? What can they show us about aging?

The great mythologist Joseph Campbell taught that fairy tales and myths were part of a single and infinitely larger story, a monomyth encoding the meaning and stages of the human adventure in the world, and a map taking us home. As we review the stories contained in this volume, we begin to see the outline of this one long and universal story, a continuous thread reaching back into the mists of time, and forward toward the far reaches of humanity's spiritual evolution. This story describes the nature and purpose of life, the challenge of aging, the power of love, and the reality of the divine world all around us.

Weaving the Stories into One

We begin our monomyth with a naive little boy previewing his journey from the protective confines of his mother's apron strings to the wide world of adults. A wise old storyteller and a little crone in an elder tree show the boy the full scope and majesty of his life's dream; he can't wait to begin the adventure.

Time goes by as our hero explores the full horizon of life - we'll leave the middle years for other fairy tale collections. He arrives, finally, at the threshold of old age. As the mature King O'Toole, he learns the art of successful aging from his soul, who brings him new insights, joys, and possibilities for his life. The king then accepts the bargain presented by Death, who asks him to surrender everything he has, gladly, and on faith alone, to restore his soul. It soon becomes apparent that an honest encounter with Death is the pivotal act of initiation transforming old age.

But the number and poignancy of losses that come with aging and death can also feel unbearably painful. Indeed, loss feels like death, for everything one takes for granted - identity, good health, and a long future - must disappear. While King O'Toole felt this great loss, Inanna, on the way to a funeral, shows us the full descent into its painful abyss. Her journey of death and rebirth applies to all of us, for aging is about loss, and grief is the secret doorway to rebirth.

Recognizing now how important death is to the journey of aging, our protagonist decides to uncover its essential secrets. He decides to confront Death himself. In his conversation with Yama, Natchiketas learns that only the self-idea dies, for consciousness, our essential nature, is beyond death. Then, discovering that all consciousness is in fact divine consciousness, Natchiketas learns who he really is. But, as Naruda found out, this kind of knowledge is easily forgotten, for the illusions of mind can re-enchant the seeker in a heartbeat. Indeed, as Owain, our protagonist must learn that the journey of awakening actually takes a long, long time, with many mistakes along the way. If we persist with sincerity and determination, however, we reach a time when enlightenment becomes more available - old age. In fact, as Rahula's story suggests, the conditions of old age are ripe not only for this development of consciousness but for the related discovery of the divine world as well.

But there is more to awakening. Kalapana risks everything to meet the goddess and feel the energy of divinity first hand. In the moment of meeting the goddess, Kalapana melts the boundaries of self and other, masculine and feminine, Heaven and Earth, sacred and profane, and experiences his own divine nature. All this allows him to live out his years in a garden paradise. His transformed consciousness has revealed Heaven on Earth and he becomes its representative.

In the conventional world of man, most of us do not reach this spiritual pinnacle of awakening, partly because fairy tales about aging as enlightenment have not yet emerged. The old man in my grandmother's parable does meet the goddess - his divine nature - but only at the very end of life. On the other hand, our concluding tale, The Color Tree, optimistically suggests that much more is waiting to be learned and integrated in this final chapter of life. In fact, maturity may offer a radically new kind consciousness and life, the implications of which can only be dimly imagined at this time in history.

The Soul and the Divine World

Our ten fairy tales have also revealed something else - something of incredible importance. They suggest that we actually live simultaneously in two worlds, the World of Man and the divine world. The World of Man is the land of ego, identity, problems and quests; the divine world is the realm of awakened consciousness inhabited by soul. Even though we may not sense its presence, divine consciousness has been with us all along, steadfastly guiding our journey and coming with help and wisdom when sincerely called.

Examples of the soul's activity are everywhere in these stories: the Little Elder-Tree Mother, King O'Toole's goose, Inanna, Luned, Pele, the angel, and my grandmother herself. These examples are women only because the stories have male protagonists (an unfortunate prejudice of history's patriarchal story tellers); it would be the reverse for female protagonists. But, as Natchiketas, Narada, and Rahula learned, the time comes when the questing male complex must itself be surrendered for the journey to proceed, and that's when the soul steps forth to lead the way to divinity and the divine world. To this end, our protagonist in the final story is an old woman and it is she who opens the perceptual gates to Heaven on Earth. Had her story continued, I suspect she would have found a strong masculine figure - her animus - to defend Garden consciousness and complete her wholeness.

All our lives, the World of Man has served as our dominant experience and frame of reference, which was particularly distressing to my grandmother. In the late life passage into old age, this balance can shift. The conventional world begins to die, the subliminal world of spirit comes to the fore, and the soul begins to whisper its divine secrets more clearly, especially about the nature of divinity and the presence of Heaven on Earth. As the mystics from across time and tradition testify, Heaven on Earth has always been here waiting for divine consciousness to open our eyes. Put another way, the higher consciousness expressed as soul cleanses and awakens our own consciousness, like the touch of the yogin, the goddess, or the night nurse, and with its pristine clarity, we see where we have always been.

The Three Secret of Aging

There is yet one more way we can summarize the experience of aging described in these tales. Hidden in our collection of stories are amazing secrets. Wherever we are on the journey, holding these secrets in mind will help us better understand our experience and navigate the road ahead. Like the magic number in Natchikas Meets Death, the secrets number three.

Secret I. Aging is an Initiation into an Extraordinary New Stage of Life

King O'Toole needed to confront Death for his initiation into spiritual maturity. He would not have experienced those extra years of creative new life had he not been willing to surrender his entire kingdom. Natchiketas, too, would not have learned the secrets of Death had he not been willing to die in his father's place and only when Narada lost everything he loved did he discover the illusion Krishna had created for him. Nor did Rahula find enlightenment until all was lost or Kalapana meet Pele until he had been repeatedly defeated. The old man in my grandmother's story had to lose his life to understand how he had betrayed his heart. And the old woman in the hospital learned the secrets of divine consciousness only after health, identity, and control were taken away. Perhaps it was Inanna who understood the three-stage nature of initiation best: 1) leaving the known world, 2) undergoing the profound and sacred ordeal of death and rebirth, and 3) returning, healed and restored, with the new values and gifts to share.

All these protagonists were initiated by loss and death. And here the equation is clear: loss = death. Each loss is a death of something; each death is the loss of something. The ego must be defeated. Then, as we give up all that we were, death initiates us into a new life. This is the central archetype of spiritual transformation. This is aging.

Secret II. Aging is a Transformation of Self and Consciousness

In their respective encounters with Death and God, Natchiketas and Narada discover that the self they had taken for granted was neither permanent nor ultimately real; instead, no matter how convincing it seemed, it was in fact a temporary creation of mind. Beneath their self-ideas shone the conscious light of divinity present in all of us.

But we have very few fairy tales explaining and depicting such profound transformations of consciousness; most are found in the enlightenment parables of the great religious figures, like Jesus, Buddha, and their followers, who surrender the self during profound mystical experiences. Though this transformation theme is ubiquitous - the phoenix of a new awakening arises from the ashes of the old self - it has not yet reformed old age. The new aging unfolding all around us, however, will change this. In exchanging personal identity for the consciousness of divinity, we will shift our allegiance from ego to divine self, giving birth to the enlightened Elder.

Secret III. Aging is the Revelation of Heaven on Earth

Owain went in search of the divine world and, after a series of epic struggles, achieved the marriage of self and soul necessary for opening his spiritual eyes to the divine world. With instruction from an awakened yogin, Rahula found the divine world in old age and, with Pele's help, Kalapana retired in paradise. In sum, as the veil of thought dissolves and divinity shines as our true nature, the radiance of Heaven on Earth appears everywhere.

In the new aging, we surrender the filters of mind that create and maintain the conventional World of Man. As the light of eternity grows brighter, it shines through reality and Heaven shines through Earth. This revelation, which marks the far reaches of humanity's spiritual evolution, holds enormous importance for humankind. While teachers from every time and religion have been telling us about this new world, only a tiny fraction of humanity has been willing to consider it. But this is changing and the enlightenment of aging will be the catalyst.

Perhaps the most profound realization in these secrets, known to mystics from every religion and era, is that we are the Creator and this world is our creation. The history of mysticism is replete with this esoteric realization - we are the One and the many. While each of us - and everything else - appears to be a separate and objective entity, the moment of illumination reveals that all are, in fact, the one Being. Put differently, phenomena, including us, are but transient versions of the One, like waves on the sea, born of divine consciousness and destined to dissolve back into it. As light is both wave and a particle, we are both human and divine, both dream and dreamer. As the mystics proclaim, the one seeking God is God.

Conclusions

It is time for humanity to wake up. Elders, willing to greet Death consciously and cheerfully, will carry the torch of enlightenment into a new world. Like the little boy in The Elder-Tree Mother seeking initiation into the great and magnificent journey of life, Elders also stand at the threshold of a great unknown. Informed with the spiritual wisdom of fairy tales and armed with secrets of initiation, transformation, and revelation, Elders can literally and profoundly change the world, not in the conventional heroic sense, but in the mystical way of awakened consciousness.

How will this change happen? The answer lies in each of us. Like kernels of corn beginning to pop in the spiritual microwave of aging, we will each contribute to a new humanity. Don't think too hard, just wake up, merge consciousness with being, and your enlightenment will show the way.

Your Story

Reflecting on your own story…

Which fairy tale speaks most personally to you? What is it telling you?

Imagining your life as a fairy tale, how might your enlightenment take place? Make up your own story of awakening.

How might the three secrets influence your attitude and experience of aging? What secret are you working on right now?

Appendices

The Hidden Meaning of Fairy Tales
And How to Understand Them

As a skyscraper must have a physical foundation many stories deep in the Earth to support it, so the human mind is built on metaphorical stories buried deep in the psyche, an archeology of human experience layered into our genes, body, mind and brain from millions of years of physical and cultural evolution. Talking to each other for countless millennia about the great and mundane experiences of life – day and night, sky and Earth, mother and father, human and animal, birth and death, love and hate, we built a communal repository of symbols and stories. We assigned and explained the significance of everything - why the sun rises, how turtle found his shell, what true love is made of, and why we suffer. Even scientific theories borrow from stories. We draw from this storehouse of archetypal imagination and meaning in every conversation.

Though varying somewhat in style and purpose, fairy tale, myth, fable, parable and legend all weave these great archetypal symbols into the stories we use to understand - or more accurately, imagine to be - the ultimate significance and purpose of the events of our life. In this way, these stories also enfold a religious or teleological intuition of the transcendent significance in the events of life that adds mystery, urgency, and importance to the journey. When someone dies, for example, we say they have gone to a better place, drawing from the universal story of an afterlife held in every culture and religion. Indeed, it is the search for the divinity, and the journey back to our true self and true home, that subliminally drives the universal story.

In this bed of collective imagination, each of us dreams an individual life, discovering how the universal story will be experienced as our own. The value of reading fairy tales and related genre resides in their ability to tell us what our life means. Their use of universal symbols awakens the part of us that instinctively understands the language of the image and archetype, potentially releasing personal insights and intuitions of profound significance to the perceptive reader. Traveling down the Road of Life, therefore, it behooves us look to these stories for compass bearings in order to understand "modern" life in general and our own struggles in particular.

Fairy tales need not be ancient to carry deep archetypal themes. Skillful storytellers use their intuitive awareness of these universal themes, albeit often unconsciously, to create new and equally enchanting tales like those my grandmother told. If a modern tale grabs you - like Charles Dickens's *A Christmas Carol* or J.K. Rowling's *Harry Potter*, it has tapped the same profound and universal themes of the human psyche. In fact, George Lucas acknowledged that he did not understand what he was trying to accomplish in *Star Wars* until he read Joseph Campbell's monumental work, *The Hero with A Thousand Faces*. The power of these new tales, therefore, lies in their creative use of ancient symbols and we all become depth psychologists as we learn to unravel them.

How to Understand Fairy Tales

Fairy tales may be approached from three levels - the literal, the symbolic and the personal. At the literal level, we read the story for sheer fun and entertainment. These are often just plain good stories filled with drama, suspense, humor, and sometimes important moral lessons, like the value of industry over sloth in Aesop's Fable The Ant and the Grasshopper.

Our interest here, however, lies more at the symbolic level where archetypes - universally recognized symbols - dwell like mythic creatures in the underground caves of the collective unconsciousness, a realm of the personality Jung believed was common to humans across all cultures and times. Simply put, we all carry the same symbolic forms hard-wired in the unconscious. Mother, Father, Child, Life, Death, Love - the list is long but we intuitively sense what each one means, and the meanings tend to be rich and nuanced. We know, for example, that the Mother symbol expresses the feminine capacity for "tender loving care," the ability to birth new life, and the prodigious generativity of the Earth, as well as darker forms such as the evil witch or step-mother.

But how do we learn to understand the strange, confusing, and fantastic ways archetypal symbols operate in fairy tales? What could a pet goose possibly tell us about aging or a tree growing in a teapot teach us about life? You already know the answer - it's hidden in your symbolic unconscious - the trick is to find ways to access your own deep knowing. That's what this book is all about, providing numerous opportunities to tap into this collective wisdom.

We are also interested in applying these symbols at the personal level to stir powerful new insights about our own lives. How do the losses of aging initiate us into a new consciousness? What has the dream of my life been about? What would happen if I woke up from that dream?

Our task, then, is to learn how to enter the symbolic realm of fairy tales to reveal their hidden meanings and apply them to our own personal experiences. A good place for the avid reader to begin is the work of mythologists and depth psychologists to observe how they use symbols, especially the more accessible works of Joseph Campbell, Allan Chinen and Robert Johnson. You also received a rich exposure to this symbolic language as we unpacked the meaning of the stories in this volume.

As you study the archetypal language of fairy tales, a lexicon of meanings will gradually expand inside you. You will see, for example, how the ocean, with its vast horizon and depth, often represents the collective unconsciousness, and how every story has a hero or heroine who must take a journey, solve a problem, defeat an obstacle, or reach a goal. These tasks engage the ego's need to master its own dark and unconscious personality forces in order to grow in consciousness, grasp the meaning of life, and awaken to the divine.

Another method for interpreting fairy tales comes directly from working with dreams, for dreams and myths come from the same unconscious depths. As Joseph Campbell explained, each dream is like a personalized myth. Tools psychotherapists employ to understand dreams, therefore, will also work with fairy tales.

Below are six approaches to understanding fairy tales taken from the art of analyzing dreams. Like the blind men feeling the elephant, each method reveals a different aspect of the whole. The goal is to use as many methods as you need to incrementally build your understanding of a symbol and its particular meaning in the story.

Free Association: Originally a psychoanalytic technique, free association asks you to write or say whatever comes to mind about a symbol or story without regard for correctness, propriety, or even relevance. The key is to avoid censoring! In this way, your unconsciousness will give you useful information though you may not understand it at first, which is OK. You will know if you are on the right track, however, when you get an "aha" feeling inside, an intuitive "yes" message.

Becoming the Symbol: A Gestalt technique, the instruction here is to imagine that you are the symbol in the dream - the monster, the car, or the shriveled lady. In your imagination, become that part, and ask yourself how you feel, what you want or need, and what you might do next.

Dialoguing with the Symbol: A similar Gestalt technique, the instruction is to have a conversation with the symbol in question. Talk to the symbol as if it were alive and conscious. Express how you feel about it, ask it questions, and allow spontaneous answers to come forth from the symbol itself, as if you were writing a dialogue between two characters. Writing down this conversation often helps it move along.

Making Up a Story about the Symbol: If this symbol was part of a story with a beginning, middle, and end, how would the story go? Be sure to include the backstory for each character or symbol. For example, how did this person grow up? Why has he come to this place? How does he solve the problem contained in the story?

Imagining the Story Going Forward: Here the goal is to imagine the story continuing. Many stories stop too soon and remain, as a result, unfinished. Imagine the story were to go on - what would happen next, and next, and next? Explore several endings, consider what each reveals, and see which ending feels most valid.

Creating an Image of the Symbol: Use art, poetry, song, or dance to create an image or experience of the symbol in question. Fill your consciousness with its energy and form to inspire or evoke an artistic expression. Let the symbol take on a life of its own to see what it wants to express.

Noticing the Detail that First Grabs Your Attention: Often, when you first hear a story, a detail will jump out at you, something quite specific. That detail represents your personal connection with, and entrance into, the story, that is, how the story has grabbed your psyche and touched some important theme or issue inside you. Now the story becomes your story. As you explore that detail, the story will come alive and pull you further into its imagery.

Researching the Meaning of the Symbol: With a dictionary of symbols or Google search, explore the definition, nature and possible meanings of a symbol and see which meanings best fit your symbol or story.

One more thing to keep in mind: Since you are the ultimate creator of meaning, every part of the story reflects a part of you. Some parts seem separate, different or alien because you defensively resist experiencing them directly, so the story expresses it as a separate entity. This is completely natural - it's a way of bringing in new information in a gradual way so you can accept it in measured doses. Experiencing each part of a fairy tale with these methods brings new insights, contributing to both self-understanding and an overall increase in consciousness.

Periwinkle Gathers Seaweed for his Mother

To illustrate these interpretive methods, I share a deceptively simple fairy tale written for me by my grandmother in 1955. It is about her little fairy named Periwinkle. I have no memory of hearing or reading this story as a child. As a young adult, however I dismissed it as sweet but rather banal - such hubris! Returning to it as an Elder, after decades of experience exploring dreams and myths, I was stunned and amazed. The message she was unconsciously giving me was profound. Follow me into this story, notice how the interpretation methods reveal an unexpected level of psychological depth and sophistication, and see how it might also say something about your life.

Just think what tiny footprints Periwinkle would make if he walked across the sand. They would be no bigger than a sandpiper's.
One day Periwinkle was walking on the sand. He had gone to the

beach to get some seaweed for his mother. She makes very good seaweed pie out of the flowers of a certain seaweed that blooms only in August. It was a hot day and Periwinkle saw with disappointment that the tide was too high to gather the seaweed, and that he would have to wait: so he lay down on the sand, and watched the gentle waves coming and going back again along the shore.

Pretty soon, two small sandpipers came hopping on the sand near Periwinkle. They were looking for tiny little fish and algae that are left as the tide goes out. At first they did not see Periwinkle they were so busy searching for food. Suddenly they found themselves right beside him. They turned, and started to run across the sand, the way sandpipers do, but Periwinkle called to them.

"Do not be afraid, sandpipers," he said. "I am your friend."

They turned and looked at him.

"We do not know you," they said. "<u>Who</u> are you and <u>what</u> are you? We have never seen anything quite like you before."

"I am Periwinkle, a little fairy," he answered. "I have come to the shore to gather seaweed for my mother. She is going to make some seaweed pie."

"Oh," said the sandpipers, "we never tasted seaweed pie; but we know that some seaweed is good to eat; and we often find tiny crabs caught in the seaweed that are very good indeed. If you wait a little while, Periwinkle, the tide will go out further, and you will have no trouble in finding all the seaweed you want."

"I will wait," said Periwinkle, and he lay down on the sand. It was a warm day and Periwinkle fell asleep.

When he woke, he saw that the tide had gone out considerably, and he walked down across the wet sand to the water's edge. There, he saw some stands of seaweed, and gathered them for his mother.

"Having any luck?" said one of the sandpipers, flying by. "Watch out for the crabs! Sometimes you will find a big crab under the seaweed; and the crabs can pinch with their claws."

"I am not afraid of crabs," said Periwinkle, and he went on boldly gathering seaweed. Now, perhaps, Periwinkle was just a little too bold. *Perhaps, he should have thought more carefully about what the sandpiper said, but Periwinkle was young and merry and having a good time, and he did not heed the sandpiper's warning. He went on gathering the seaweed, without taking the trouble to look out for the crabs.*

Periwinkle saw a bunch of seaweed at the water's edge and waded in to pull it out. Just then a big crab crawled out of the seaweed. Periwinkle was so surprised, for a moment he could scarcely move. Then he tuned to run toward the shore, but the sand was wet, and he slipped and fell. Before he could regain his balance the big crab was by his side. Periwinkle rolled over to get away, but before he could get up, the crab's claw caught one of his wings - and Periwinkle could not get away. Poor Periwinkle was a very frightened fairy. He did not know what to do. The crab held him fast, and started to drag him down into the water.

What would have happened to Periwinkle I do not know if one of the sandpipers had not flown by just then. He saw Periwinkle and he gave a cry of alarm that sandpipers give when they are frightened. Other sandpipers heard the cry and flew to where Periwinkle was. Then the two sandpipers, who had become Periwinkle's friends, did a very brave thing. They flew down over the crab and pecked at his shell, though even the pecking did not make him loosen his hold on Periwinkle's wing.

Just then a boy came by. He wondered what all those sandpipers were doing together by the water's edge. He ran down to see, and he came so fast, splashing into the water as he ran, that the crab was frightened, and let go of Periwinkle's wing. Then the crab crawled quickly into the water and swam away. Poor Periwinkle lay trembling on the sand. He cried because his wing hurt him where the crab had pinched it.

"Well I never - " said the boy as he looked at Periwinkle. *"Who are you?"*

"I am a fairy," answered Periwinkle. *"Do not hurt me."*

"I will not hurt you," said the boy. *"Are you what the crab had in*

his claw?"

"Yes," said Periwinkle. "He had hold of my wing."

"Lucky you escaped," said the boy. "Can I help you?"

"I think I am all right," said Periwinkle. "When the pain is less in my shoulder I can get up and fly home."

"Are you an honest to goodness fairy?" said the boy. "I thought fairies only lived in story books. I never expected to see one."

"Sometimes boys and girls see fairies," said Periwinkle.

"Well I never did," said the boy again. "What were you doing on the beach? Were you going swimming?"

"No," said periwinkle. "I was gathering seaweed for my mother. She makes very good seaweed pie."

"Seaweed pie! I never heard of that," said the boy. "Is it good to taste?"

"Very good," said Periwinkle. Periwinkle got to his feet rather stiffly; his shoulder ached. "I must pick up the seaweed now that I have gathered," he said.

"Well, well," said the boy. "I never expected to see a fairy. I wonder if I am awake or dreaming. What is your name?"

"Periwinkle is my name. What is yours, boy?"

"My name is Jack," said the boy.

Just then a voice called from the bluff above the shore.

"Hurry up Jack! It is time for lunch."

It was Jack's father calling.

"Good-bye fairy," said Jack. "I must go. I hope I will see you again."

"You will," said Periwinkle.

Jack ran up the bluff to his father's car.

Periwinkle started to gather the seaweed he had dropped when the crab caught him, but his shoulder hurt him, and it was hard work. The sandpipers, who had flown away when the boy came running on the sand, flew back to Periwinkle.

"Are you all right Periwinkle?" they said. "You gave us all a terrible fright!"

"I am right enough," said Periwinkle, "but my shoulder still aches."

"Let us help you gather the seaweed," said the sandpipers; and they helped Periwinkle pick up the strands of seaweed that he had dropped when he saw the crab. Periwinkle thanked them, and with his arm full of seaweed, he tried to fly. It was very hard work, because his shoulder ached, but he managed to get into the air, and back to his mother. She put him to bed to rest, and made a brew of healing herbs to put on his shoulder.

After a few days of rest, Periwinkle's shoulder was well, and he could fly with ease; but he never gathered seaweed again without looking carefully to see if any big crabs were near by.

Interpretation

Beginning with free association, I let my mind wander uncensored about the opening theme: a little boy goes off to the beach alone to find seaweed for his mother. As an adult and a parent, I wondered first whether Periwinkle was sent by his mother or ventured out on his own, for it seems a little dangerous to permit a young child - or little fairy - to play alone at the seashore. Then I realized that this ambiguity did not really matter in the story, because every boy must one day leave the safety of his mother's side to go out in to the big, wide world. Stunned, I understood that my grandmother had written a coming-of-age story for me.

Drawing next from depth psychology, I recalled that the ocean often symbolizes humanity's vast collective unconscious filled with all the possibilities of life's great journey. Periwinkle has come to the threshold of this vastness, though he is still too young to begin his journey into the world. As a vulnerable little fairy, he embodies what Jung called the *puer* archetype - the naïve and dreamy little boy who lives in the imaginary world of fantasy and superheroes prior to adolescence, just as I was at nine.

Periwinkle has come to the ocean to collect seaweed for his mother's pie, suggesting that she will feed him elements of the unconscious in a safe and prepared way, like pureed baby food. Falling asleep on the shore similarly reflects a childlike response to the awe-inspiring vastness of the sea, as an infant falls asleep anywhere implicitly assuming he will be safe and protected. Naive and trusting, Periwinkle approaches the story's characters as friends and boldly declares (as an imaginary little superhero might) that their crab warning does not frighten him.

Although they are birds, sandpipers do not fly much; rather they stay close to the ground and run in and out of waves as they search for food. In this way, they move easily between the edge of the World of Man and the unconscious. They are relatively small and defenseless birds, again synonymous with youth, but at least they are focused on the actual reality around them, keeping them from danger. This attitude of wary caution is exactly what Periwinkle lacks, hinting that he has not developed this capacity for himself. As a result, the crab catches Periwinkle unprepared. Looking back, I sense that my grandmother saw this same innocence and naïve bravery in me, prompting a cautionary tale.

What might the crab symbolize? Ask yourself that question and for a moment see what comes up in your free associations. Coming out of the ocean, threatening to pull him back into it, the crab might first symbolize the regressive pull of an unconscious complex, keeping him from growing up, fitting given his puer nature. The crab's hard shell and exoskeleton imply a primitive life form on the evolutionary scale, suggesting perhaps an equally primitive complex, and one that can be particularly aggressive with its huge claws. What could that primitive part be in a child? My association is to a young child's primitive capacity for aggression - like biting, pinching, or hitting, aggression that will re-emerge in adolescence to help him break his maternal dependence and move into the world. Perhaps both interpretations are appropriate, for aggression is regressive if turned against normal development - the "I don't want to grow up" complex - or healthy when it becomes an energy for individu-ation.

To gather more information, I began a dialogue with this crab:

Me: Crab, you are scary to a little person. You are so well defended in your shell. What do you want?

Crab: I want to be left alone. I was going about my business when Periwinkle pulled the seaweed off me and I reacted instinc-tively. Then I thought he was food and wanted to take him back into the sea.

Me: OK, but why didn't you turn him loose? He was a fairy.

Crab: I was hungry. That's how the world works. Animals eat each other. It is a reality principle. You're too old to be naïve.

Me: Wow. You're right. This is how the world works. This is what Periwinkle - or me as a little boy - needs to learn to break free from maternal dependency. The world is dangerous and adolescents need experience with aggression to grow strong and independent.

To take my understanding a little deeper, I imagined that I was the crab, letting myself become the symbol. If I were that crab, I would be feeling pretty "crabby." I can hear myself saying, "Leave me alone! I have work to do. I have to survive. I wear this shell because I am actually pretty small and vulnerable myself inside. People love to catch and eat crabs like me. So I keep to myself and I can bury myself in the sand and hide in between feedings. So go away and stop assuming you know me. It's as dangerous for me as for the fairy."

This is another interesting discovery - it's the same theme in a different guise. As a nine-year-old little boy, I too am soft and shy on the inside, but I don't have much of a shell or claw to protect myself from the hard side of human relationships. Perhaps that's what the crab is showing me - a testy, immature part of myself prior to adolescence that needs to develop into masculine strength. But a crab never becomes very social and if my capacity for aggression remains concealed behind an immature dependency or desire for solitude, I will not grow up. I will become what the Jungians call a *puer aeternus* - someone like Peter Pan who refuses to surrender his little boy innocence and freedom.

Returning to the story, we see that solution to this developmental dilemma arrives in the form of a real boy, one old enough to stop believing in fairies and trade the world of childish imagination for the world of real people and events. It is the boy who saves Periwinkle from the "hermit" crab, showing him by example how to be forceful and aggressive in a healthy and constructive way. Moreover, the boy arrives from the world of men, for his father is nearby, confirming that this developmental threshold calls the boy to move from the early maternal dependency of childhood to the adolescent independence of young men.

If this were a dream and I wanted to make up a story about it, I would say it was about a dependent little boy who came to the ocean unconsciously looking for initiation into manhood. Boys in all cultures search for initiation in play, risk-taking, and male bravado. Of course Periwinkle is too young to make this transition, but he is instinctively drawn to it. When I begin to dream the story forward, I quickly imagine myself getting well from my injury and playing outside with male friends - getting more physical in sports, pursuing adventures with guy friends in the wider world, and beginning exploring relationships with girls. It felt good to moving into my masculinity and discovering its strengths, energies, and potentials. Grounded in my new "man" body, my fairy wings would fall off one day unnoticed.

Next, research on the meaning of initiation as a symbol provided another interesting parallel. For those indigenous peoples who formally initiate their youth, coming-of-age rites always involves an element of danger and often a wound (in fact, in many cultures, that wound was circumcision), and Periwinkle certainly experiences both. But as I said, he is still too young for this passage, so instead he goes home to his mother who puts him to bed.

Next, the detail that grabbed me personally in this story was the lack of supervision from the mother. I wondered a lot about whether she understood the risk Periwinkle assumed going to the ocean alone. My own mother seemed to believe that her sons needed little or no protection; in fact she seemed to overlook our dependency needs altogether. The story, in other words, spoke directly to my own feeling of maternal unavailability and the complicated relationship I subsequently had with her.

Finally, the interpretive method I did not illustrate here was to artistically create an image of the dream or symbol. Had I done so, I think I would have drawn a boy leaving home like Huck Finn to join older boys in the great adventure of life.

Conclusions

My grandmother's simple story about a little fairy collecting seaweed for his mother came to symbolize the upcoming challenging of adolescence. Unbeknownst to me, she was acting as wise old crone warning me to be alert and ready, for adolescence is fraught with developmental dangers not the least of which is refusing to grow up and enter the rough-and-tumble world of masculinity. She was telling me that emancipation from my mother and movement into the world of boys and men would be the developmental task of adolescence, and that even though this transition was a few years off, I should begin to anticipate it. Did my grandmother realize she was communicating such a deep and psychologically complex issue to me? Probably not, but talented storytellers need not be depth psychologists to create tales that intuitively speak the themes of the listener.

Throughout *Bedtime Stories for Elders*, I blend these interpretation methods rather casually, and emphasize the universal themes and meanings rather then my personal intuitions, for these tales are meant for you. You are encouraged, however, to apply all these methods to the stories to make them your own.

Finally the perceptive reader might ask how this story of childhood initiation relates to our theme of fairy tales for enlightened Elders. I believe it does and the key is the symbol of initiation. We are initiated again and again in life with each new developmental stage and, as we saw, aging is itself an initiation of immense importance. Just as Periwinkle did, we too move from one world to another, and in aging we travel from the middle-age realm of work, identity, ambition, and family, to the twilight world of mystery and enlightenment.

Sources

The Little Elder-Tree Mother. Anderson, Hans Christian. (1893). Hans Christian Anderson's Stories for Households. McLoughlin Brothers: Google Books.

King O'Toole and his Goose. Jacobs, Joseph. (Ed.). (1990). Celtic Fairy Tales. London: Bracken Books.

Living the Myth of Inanna. Robinson, John. Living the Myth of Inanna, Psychological Perspectives, C.G. Jung Institute of Los Angeles, Vol. 48: 110-120, 2005.

Natchiketa Meets Death. Mascaro, Juan. (Translator). (1965). The Upanishads. London: Penguin Books.

Fetch Me A Cup of Water. A teaching story frequently told in both Buddhist and Hindu traditions. Retold from recollection.

The Lady and the Fountain. Zimmer, Heinrich. (1973). The King and the Corpse. New Jersey: Princeton University Press.

Rahula Eclipses Age. Robinson, James (Trans). (1979). Buddha's Lions. Berkeley: Dharma Publishing.

Meeting the Goddess. Yolen, Jane. (1999). Gray Heroes. New York: Penguin Books.

Periwinkle Meets the Old Man. Adams, Agnes Claflin. (2001). Periwinkle: Fairy Stories for My Grandchildren. Cambridge: Claflin Family Press.

The Color Tree. Robinson, John. Written expressly for this book.

Also by John Robinson

Death of a Hero, Birth of the Soul
But Where Is God? Psychotherapy and the Religious Search
Ordinary Enlightenment
Finding Heaven Here
The Three Secrets of Aging

BOOKS

O is a symbol of the world, of oneness and unity. In different cultures it also means the "eye," symbolizing knowledge and insight. We aim to publish books that are accessible, constructive and that challenge accepted opinion, both that of academia and the "moral majority."

Our books are available in all good English language bookstores worldwide. If you don't see the book on the shelves ask the bookstore to order it for you, quoting the ISBN number and title. Alternatively you can order online (all major online retail sites carry our titles) or contact the distributor in the relevant country, listed on the copyright page.

See our website **www.o-books.net** for a full list of over 500 titles, growing by 100 a year.

And tune in to myspiritradio.com for our book review radio show, hosted by June-Elleni Laine, where you can listen to the authors discussing their books.

MySpiritRadio